THE ORIGINS OF NOSTALGIA

THE ORIGINS OF NOSTALGIA

Memories and Reflections

SVETLANA BOYM

EDITED BY RON ROBERTS

BLOOMSBURY ACADEMIC
NEW YORK · LONDON · OXFORD · NEW DELHI · SYDNEY

BLOOMSBURY ACADEMIC
Bloomsbury Publishing Inc
1385 Broadway, New York, NY 10018, USA
50 Bedford Square, London, WC1B 3DP, UK
29 Earlsfort Terrace, Dublin 2, Ireland

BLOOMSBURY, BLOOMSBURY ACADEMIC and the Diana logo are
trademarks of Bloomsbury Publishing Plc

First published in the United States of America 2022
This paperback edition published 2023

Copyright © Estate of Svetlana Boym, 2022

Introduction © Ronald Anthony Roberts, 2022

The following works are published here by permission of the Estate of Svetlana Boym:
"Cosmos in the Girls' Washroom"
"Children, We've Been Deceived!"
"The Secret Life of a Communal Apartment Neighbor"
"Tearing Away"
"Sasha, Misha, Napoleon and Josephine (circa 1992)"
"Replace the Irreplaceable! A Tale of Immigrant Objects"
"My Significant Others: Zenita, Susana, Ilanka"

The following works are quoted with attribution. Whilst every effort has been
made to locate copyright holders, the publishers would be grateful
to hear from any person(s) not here acknowledged.
Vladimir Vysotsky, "Pesenka o pereselenii dush" (Song of the Soul's Transmigration").
Bulat Okudzhava, "Dezhurny po apreliu" ("A Patrolman of April").
Vladimir Vysotsky, "Ona byla v Parizhe" ("She'd Been to Paris").
Vladimir Vysotsky, "Ban'ka po Belomu" ("Heat the Banya").
Bulat Okudzhava, "I'm writing a historical novel."

For legal purposes the Acknowledgments on p. 156 constitute an
extension of this copyright page.

Cover design by Eleanor Rose
Cover image: Flowers on a granite memorial plaque at the Bratsk Cemetery in memory of
the fallen Soviet soldiers of the 2nd World War © Aleksandr Zubkov / Getty Images

All rights reserved. No part of this publication may be reproduced or transmitted
in any form or by any means, electronic or mechanical, including photocopying,
recording, or any information storage or retrieval system, without prior
permission in writing from the publishers.

Bloomsbury Publishing Inc does not have any control over, or responsibility for, any
third-party websites referred to or in this book. All internet addresses given in this
book were correct at the time of going to press. The author and publisher regret
any inconvenience caused if addresses have changed or sites have ceased
to exist, but can accept no responsibility for any such changes.

Library of Congress Cataloging-in-Publication Data
Names: Boym, Svetlana, 1959–2015, author. | Roberts, Ron, 1955–, editor.
Title: The origins of nostalgia: memories and reflections / Svetlana Boym; edited by Ron Roberts.
Description: New York: Bloomsbury Academic, 2022. | Includes bibliographical references and index. |
Summary: "The final unpublished works of the late philosopher, cultural critic and media artist,
Svetlana Boym, The Origins of Nostalgia comprises a series of autobiographical reflections which provide
unique insights and background to Boym's existing body of work"—Provided by publisher.
Identifiers: LCCN 2021048723 (print) | LCCN 2021048724 (ebook) | ISBN 9781501389931
(hardback) | ISBN 9781501389979 (paperback) | ISBN 9781501389948 (epub)
| ISBN 9781501389955 (pdf) | ISBN 9781501389962 (ebook other)
Subjects: LCSH: Boym, Svetlana, 1959–2015. | Boym, Svetlana, 1959–2015—Childhood and youth. |
Slavists—Biography. | Computer artists—Biography. | Immigrants—Soviet Union—Biography. |
Nostalgia. | Soviet Union—Social life and customs. | LCGFT: Autobiographies.
Classification: LCC PS3602.O974 Z46 2022 (print) | LCC PS3602.O974 (ebook) |
DDC 814/.54 [B]–dc23/eng/20211117
LC record available at https://lccn.loc.gov/2021048723
LC ebook record available at https://lccn.loc.gov/2021048724

ISBN:	HB:	978-1-5013-8993-1
	PB:	978-1-5013-8997-9
	ePDF:	978-1-5013-8995-5
	ePUB:	978-1-5013-8994-8

Typeset by Integra Software Services Pvt. Ltd.

To find out more about our authors and books visit www.bloomsbury.com
and sign up for our newsletters.

For Musa and Yury Goldberg

Photograph of Svetlana in her Cambridge home. © Estate of Svetlana Boym. Used with permission.

CONTENTS

Introduction: *"Snippets of experience"* 1

1 Cosmos in the Girls' Washroom 5

2 Children, We've Been Deceived! 17

3 The Secret Life of a Communal Apartment Neighbor 39

4 Tearing Away 65

5 Sasha, Misha, Napoleon and Josephine (circa 1992) 85

6 Replace the Irreplaceable! A Tale of Immigrant Objects 103

7 My Significant Others: Zenita, Susana, Ilanka 115

Acknowledgments 156
Index 157

Introduction

"Snippets of experience"

> Having grown up in a "communal apartment," I inherited some of my grandparents' and neighbors' stories.
> —(SVETLANA BOYM 2017: 138)

Marcel Proust wrote that "The only true voyage of discovery, the only fountain of Eternal Youth, would be not to visit strange lands but to possess other eyes, to behold the universe through the eyes of another." All of Svetlana Boym's writings are testimony to her unwavering capacity to see the world afresh—to render familiar what was hitherto strange and to make of the familiar, something vibrant and new. In her life and work, she straddled both Eastern and Western thought at a crucial historical moment, taking full creative advantage of her situation to prize open our understanding of the cultural flux which has so far defined the twenty-first century. It is a critical moment of global nostalgia which may either mark a pause in the collective human venture, a staging post for looking back to past hopes or possibly a point of inflexion before darker times. Then again, Svetlana always blinked at such binary thinking—invoking the imperatives of the Soviet avant-garde writer Viktor Shklovsky's third way as the impossible option which must be taken.

The pieces collected here, all autobiographical or semi-autobiographical, "snippets of experience" as Svetlana would describe them, capture her penchant for seamlessly melding, poetically and dream-like at times, the intensively personal with the everyday and the world-historical. We can see in several of the accounts the formative conditions for the thinking which she was to develop later. They provide glimpses of a childhood and young adulthood in Leningrad/St. Petersburg that was in creative spirited revolt with the stifling conditions and imposed utopia of totalitarian rule, the everyday conditions of which are still poorly understood in the floundering Western democracies. We ignore this knowledge at our peril. Included here is a piece "Tearing Away" (translated from the Russian by one of Svetlana's students Maria Vassileva and with an introduction by her childhood friend Natal'ya Strugach) written by Svetlana in Leningrad in 1981, a time when she was excluded from Herzen University, Leningrad and was awaiting permission to leave the Soviet Union. In its evocative and melancholic tone can be detected the relentless daily grind of a system of social control, fraying at the edges and dying in slow motion. Beyond observations on the Kafkaesque dimensions of Soviet life and bureaucracy we also see here the importance of friendships, familial and otherwise, which contributed to Svetlana's flourishing and to her always humane, if occasionally ironic, outlook on the world.

Anthropologists and psychologists have enabled us to see that through memory people don't just recall the world, they actively rebuild it and recreate it and hence, the past never ceases to be in flux. For readers familiar with Svetlana Boym's work and for those new to it, these stories will enable what has gone before to be viewed in a different light. The reconstruction of the past permits a window to be opened to different futures and to a different relationship with the world and its peoples.

In his *Book of Embraces*, Eduardo Galeano provides us with a brief allegorical tale—of a world which "is a heap of people, a sea of tiny flames," each of which shines with his or her own light. No two flames are alike. There are big flames and little flames, flames of every colour. Some people's flames are so still they don't even flicker in the wind, while others have wild flames that fill the air with sparks. Some foolish flames neither burn nor shed light, but others blaze with life so fiercely that you can't look at them without blinking and if you approach, you shine in fire.

Svetlana's flame blazed fiercely and with fun, rooted to the earth, elegant and assured. It was a pleasure to know her and a pleasure to edit these works which she has left to us.

Ron Roberts

References

Boym, S. (2017) *The Off-Modern*. London. Bloomsbury Academic.
Galeano, E. (1992) *Book of Embraces*. New York. Norton. The quote is from *The World*, 15.
Proust, M. (1913/2003) *In search of lost time*, vol. 5. London. Penguin.

1

Cosmos in the Girls' Washroom

One of the first things I learned how to draw in the kindergarten was a cosmic rocket. I was bad at drawing anything from real life, like cats, dogs, people or buildings. But the rocket was different. Using all of the available colored pencils, from red to gold, I pictured fairy tale vehicles with bright flames shooting from its tails and the proud "USSR" written on its body. Poised between heaven and Earth, my colorful rockets ecstatically defied the force of gravity. Other kids loved rockets too. Our urban playgrounds were strewn by the small rockets; we would slide down their shafts and then climb back up again and again, building true friendships on the way, until our anxious parents interrupted our games with their little adult concerns about our food, cold and safety.

Born at the time of the Soviet cosmic triumph in space, my generation was supposed to look at the world as if from outer space. The word sputnik, Russian for "satellite," means a "companion," or even, a "significant other." Indeed, Sputnik, first launched in 1957, was one of our first companions and favorite toys. We did not dream of becoming doctors and lawyers, but cosmonauts (or, if the worse came to the worst, geologists). We were encouraged to aim upward and not westward. Indeed, a trip to the Moon seemed more likely than a journey to America:

"Would you like to have a million?" asked the lead singer.

"No!" answered a chorus of Soviet children.

"Would you like to go to the Moon?"

"Yes!"

The cosmic journey was to be a joyful emigration, upwards, not westwards. It might cost a million (dollars) now, but then it was free. Every fairy tale we read in our early childhood spoke to us about a journey far away, to St. Elsewhere or into the Kosmos. Whenever the Russian hero Ivan the Fool found himself on the crossroads, ordered to go "there nobody knows where" to find "that nobody knows what," we suspected that he had traveled into space, just like Gagarin.

The American term "outer space" refers to something contiguous to Earth, a new frontier—not so much the wild West, but the wild sky. The Soviet notion of cosmos, on the other hand, comes from the Greek, meaning "order, ornament, harmony," and suggests a harmonized chaos, where human or divine presence is made manifest. The word Cosmos links Soviet space technology with the mystic theories of Russian cosmism from the late nineteenth century, it was part of a history of technology, an enchanted technology, founded on charisma as much as calculus, on pre-modern myth as well as modern science, In the exploration of the cosmos, science merged with science fiction, and ideology sounded like poetry.

In the 1950s and 1960s Soviet advances in space exploration were directly linked to the advent of Communism: "This generation of Soviet citizens will live in the era of Communism," proclaimed the New Program of the Communist Party on July 30, 1961. Only three months earlier, on April 12, 1961, the first man flew into space, Yuri Gagarin (1934–1968), the exemplary Soviet citizen of the future, became known all over the world for his larger-than-life smile, framed in the halo of a space helmet. When Gagarin made his flight, the Soviet Union was about to proclaim itself the winner of the Cold War. His triumph in the cosmos promised a victory over time and space, ensuring a radiant future and the transcendence of all earthly hardships.

In the world of our childhood there was no individual death. The war heroes committed heroic feats, but that was different. I remember how I asked what happened to the first animal sent into space, a dog with the most common name "Laika." We were never told that Laika didn't come back, or even worse, wasn't meant to come back. It's hard to write this, but Laika ... died. And the same happened to the immortal Yuri Gagarin. In 1968 he died tragically in what appeared to be a routine training accident, incommensurable with his successful cosmic journey. Extraordinary cosmic achievement was followed by ordinary earthly negligence. After Gagarin's death, a popular female star sang a love song for him, addressing the cosmonaut with the intimate "you:"

The earth is empty without you.
How can I survive these lonely hours?
Only the stars share with you their tenderness.

This cosmic romance, however, did not survive our teenage years. The seeds of its demise date back to the late 1960s, but by the 1970s we started to prefer the yellow submarine of a smuggled Beatles album to yet another rocket, which seemed to fly only on the front page of the newspaper *Pravda*. Like the cosmonaut himself, the dream of cosmos proved mortal.

By the time we became teenagers, rumors about the human and animal victims of the Soviet space program, always shrouded in secrecy, abounded. It was as if the exploration of black holes within the universe aimed to cover up the black spots of Soviet history.

With some trepidation I realize that we were the generation that was supposed to live in the era of communism and travel to the moon. We did not fulfill our mission. Instead we were forced to confront the ruins of utopia; eventually, we discovered mortality and went westwards, not upwards.

My father became a communist right after Yuri Gagarin's flight into space; by his own admission, the decision to enter the Party was his only way to secure for me a place in his factory's kindergarten, otherwise I would have to be abandoned to my own devices or to the transient babysitters.

In the absence of religious holidays, the rhythm of our year rolled around the revolutionary holidays that were also seasonal and vaguely winked at their religious predecessors. The main one was the secular "New Year" (January 1, all Union party—not surprisingly now it's a three-week holiday that includes Western and Eastern Christmas and New Year according to the Old and New calendar. Those who celebrate Chanukah or Crazy Kwantza keep quiet now and celebrate whatever comes). Then there were minor Winter and Spring festivities—the Day of the Soviet Army, Men's day February 23 and the International Women's Day, March 8 and the Day of the Soviet Aviation, April 12. The main revolutionary holidays, May 1 and November 7, were marked with public demonstrations and military parades. As kids we were dragged to the demonstrations with a promise of meager fun and lots of obligatory-voluntary rituals. My father occasionally volunteered to carry a big banner from early morning till late in the evening—for this service to the Party he could get a day off for his vacation and could stand on one of those prop-mobiles carrying heroic stage sets. There is a faded color photo of me next to a partially lit Cosmic map. I am wearing my fake-fur hat that looks like a cosmic helmet, age ten or so. I look very serious, as always, with heavy Brezhnev-style eyebrows, not yet trimmed. There are colorful non-cosmic balloons in my hand and I look like I am elsewhere, perhaps, dreaming of being lifted out of the whole demonstration as soon as possible but not before we sing a catchy song together which must be "The March of the Aviators:"

> We were born to make fairy tales come true,
> to conquer distances and space.
> Reason gave us steel wings for arms
> and a flaming motor for a heart.

The strange inflated motor of the heart in the first couplet jeopardized the journey of the Soviet Icarus. Never practice this at home kids! Don't inflate anything. If you do, don't fly outside, please, at least not literally. Remember best flying vehicles were for dreams only.

So, what were we supposed to do with this immense energy of cosmic dreaming—so misdirected? What happened to that cosmic drive in the country of "scientific atheism" with no religious education whatsoever?

Discouraged by ideology that took over even Gagarin's shy smile, we looked for sly ways towards the absolute. My unofficial search for cosmic encounters moved from disillusionment to wonder. In the last years of my high school in Leningrad there was a fashion to have spiritualist séances like in the literary salons of the late nineteenth century and with it came interest in the occult and cosmic with a small "c." Kycha and I decided to organize one such séance in her non-communal apartment when her family was away. We set little plates on the wet table around the letters and I could just swear the plates shivered a little. But how to read that elusive wet rift? Can we replicate it when our friends will come? Thriving for success in matters spiritual and cosmic usually prepares you for a failure.

Kycha didn't want to leave things to fickle chance. So, she suggested that in case the spirits are not in the mood for dialogue, I could use an empty glass and mumble something. I could be the spirit of, Lermontov, for example. The choice was mine.

All the girls gathered in a somber and mysterious mood. There was some trepidation in the room. They called for poets and cosmonauts. The spirit of Yuri Gagarin seemed angry. The arrow advanced towards the letter "W" but stopped right there. The poets didn't yield our address either. Then Kycha gave me a hint and I began to woo into the empty glass: "I am a sp—iiii—rii-t of Lermontov." "It's boring and sad and no respite from life's travails."

The evening was a success and I never came out of the closet. But as a result, I lost trust in cosmic communication for a while. How can you speak to the Kosmos through the empty glass? It made me sad; the cheater got cheated out of the cosmic experience.

The same year we had a very different experience of cosmic learning that involved no impersonation and no images.

We had one unusual teacher in my high school who prided herself on attending Leningrad University. Her specialization was in Marxist-Leninist critiques of Western Intellectual history. Our history had a clear master plot and a Hollywood happy ending. Only at the end, the boy didn't get the girl (or the other way around), but still everyone lived happily thereafter in the radiant future. After the bumpy road, there was the light at the end of the tunnel, Scientific Socialism and Communism, a Classless Society, from everyone according to ability, to everyone according to their needs, Scientific Atheism, Paradise on Earth, victory over the West, roundtrips to the Kosmos, almost as easy as the early trips to the Crimea.

We already knew the master plot and the critique, so we were most interested in what was most criticized. We hung on the teacher's lips hoping to gain access to the forbidden knowledge. This time the bad guy was very glamorous, mysterious and politically incorrect—"subjective idealism." The eccentric seventeenth-century philosopher George Berkeley believed that maybe the world is immaterial and doubted the existence of everyday objects as well as abstract concepts. Are this table and chair near us real, or mere tricks of color and light? Maybe they only exist in our minds? Perception was the key word. We don't know anything beyond our perception. Imagine how exciting is that?? No big words: School, Motherland, Blackboard, Communism, Capitalism. No tall guy with pimples who doesn't return your gaze—it's all perception!!

I couldn't contain myself. I lost a sense of my bodily limits. I was closing and opening my eyes, pinching myself, excited to suddenly come into direct touch with my perception. I must have written a secret note to Kycha. Immediately after the class we ran to the only private place in the whole damned school building that probably had broken listening devices. There we could get a little peace and quiet and just think it over. No, we didn't sit on the toilets; the stalls were opened. We sat on the windowsill; on the threshold between inside and outside. Luckily most girls ran around the corridor flirting with guys in the intermission and neglecting natural needs. We immediately voted to create The Club of Subjective Idealists, Salut, George Berkeley! We were so happy that Berkeley stood up to Newtonian certainty. Hey, did the apple really fall on your head or was it all in your head already? The little worm of an English migraine crawling out of the fruit's heart in the uncertain twilight?

"Wait," asked Kycha, "what about us, do we exist?" Yes, yes, I thought. Exist we must, at least for the duration of this cold afternoon in the girls' washroom. For if we didn't exist, who would question our existence?

I recall little of the rituals of the Club of Subjective Idealists. Perhaps it had none. Our world was defamiliarized. Victor Shklovsky had already invented his *o-stranenie* but we didn't know it yet and Berkeley was our first step towards it. We got a break from the master plot. George Berkeley led us into philosophy through a side corridor of mind-shattering immaterialism; a shadow play of real and unreal. No synthesis was possible, however many diagrams you're willing to draw on the blackboard. The blackboard melts under your chalk like spring earth filled with worms and weeds. It's March out, no Soviet holidays in sight, no May First demonstrations, no banners with neon profiles of dead cosmonauts, no larger-than-life Lenin and Brezhnev. Immaterialism triumphs. We walk out of school in dirty Leningrad sleet to doubt our drab teenage life and catch the sun blinks with the sun blink net of our imagination. We won't hold them in captivity for too long, just play and let go.

That philosophy of light and perception dubbed "subjective idealism" was a liberating road, off-Enlightenment. For me it was about the tricks of light, not total illumination; artistic lucidity, not didactic elucidation. Later, it might have found its serpentine way into serious art and philosophy, influencing avant-garde theories of light and even Albert Einstein. I learnt though that Berkeley briefly traveled to New England and hoped to build Palladian architecture in Rhode Island. He was a genial and cosmopolitan eccentric who might have not expected the following in the Leningrad washroom. But did he really exist?

That mysterious flicker of light opened a fissure into the universe through which we connected to other sympathetic worlds, non-contemporaneous with ours.

A year later I had my most significant cosmic encounter. It happened during a physics class. Usually I listened to our mildly dim-witted but generally good-natured physics teacher in a distracted fashion. I liked theory but experiments always failed me. That was the class like no other. It was the time of the freezing Leningrad thaw.

"Good morning, pupils," she said. "Today's topic: The Universe." And then she read in a dull and deadpan tone of voice as she always did:

"Point one: The Universe is unmeasurable and infinite.: *Vselennaia beschislenna i beskonechna*."

Vselennaia beschislenna i beskonechna

I could hear the blood flowing in my body. I listened no more. Vselennaia beschislenna I beskonechna. I was outside time and space.

Whispering, haunting, promising, mysterious, ineffable consonants— *chisssle skonechhhhn vsellennannan*

It was a poem, but more than a poem—vssssbschhh—the birth of the poem from the spirit of primordial *shimmer*.

Chichichi—nnnna ... nechnnnnnnaa ....vs—a cosmic kiss, a breath ... and then a melodic accord—na, na! The Universe was humming in my head and I could embrace the cosmos as long as I closed my eyes.

I never remember what happens before and after an important event. That moment in the physics class had a long duration of time, melodious, folding, shimmering. Who cares for the plot? There was no before and after, no how, what or so what. Even the best investigative journalist wouldn't be able to get out of me what I did coming out of class; did I hustle with other kids finding my winter coat thrown in the communal heap, looking for my hateful warm trousers and a burgundy hat with a tussle? Then I might have walked home on Kirov Avenue past the empty store called "Shoes" which sold medium-heel pumps with prim bows that could have been worn by the first woman cosmonaut Valentina Tereshkova twenty years earlier. I ran by the closed movie theater "Ars" with the poster for an old Italian movie blowing in the wind and bravely walked into the secret passage of interconnected yards that only street kids knew. I can hang the scenery around like an amateur theater director with rags from 1970s Leningrad underground art, half-finished abstractions grey on grey, or surrealist beaks on top of naked girls (the artist died from unknown causes on the eve of perestroika.) Or if you prefer, I borrow a stylish candle from Sir George Berkeley and give the scene some classical depth, the dignified Palladio style room, spacious and airy, just the way he dreamed it, not far from me now, in Newport, Rhode Island.

Vselenna beshchislenna i beskonechna. There was something euphoric and unspeakable there. A teenage sublime. It stayed with me because it didn't have a name. It didn't inscribe into anything, wasn't circumscribed by it. Perhaps, my photographs, not words, capture that wonder and flicker of light.

****

My private Kosmos lay hidden somewhere inside me. I was uneasy with big words, afraid to overshadow the mystery with the official heroics. In the meantime, as we were growing up the cosmic heroes were dying out and the story of the Soviet Kosmos was turning into a tragic parable. Cosmic exploration began as a philosophical and scientific quest for free space and the defiance of earthly gravitation; it culminated in a Soviet mega-industry that made dreams come true and, inadvertently, put an end to all collective dreaming.

The Soviet rocket underwent a metamorphosis of scale and power. First it was a dream image and a scientific fantasy, the small model rocket invented by Tsiolkovsky and designed by Korolev. The model paved the way for the actual construction of space technology. The rocket became the larger-than-life vehicle to the glorious future; it was supposed to conquer space and make the Soviet Union the most powerful country in the world. The myth of cosmos came to an end together with the dissolution of the Soviet Union, or perhaps even earlier. It was the last utopia in which science, ideology and dreams worked together in an attempt to break loose from the dystopian human condition. The Soviet space program is no longer the model of the future but a souvenir of the past. By the end of the twentieth century, the cosmos had turned from a futuristic utopia into a space for nostalgic remembrance.

The conquest of space changed our perception of Earth; the journey into space made possible the concept of a "global village." Today's fantasies do not unfold in the heavenly heights but in the virtual dimensions of the Internet. Hardly a space of wonder and sublimity, of immortality and immensity, it nevertheless supports the faith in technological progress and a new illusion of infinity. It is based on big data, not big dreams. As for the Soviet fairy tale, it ended as mysteriously as it began. Ivan the Fool, the Soviet Icarus, was not burnt by the sun but rather by his earthly circumstances. We are still not entirely sure if he went "there nobody knows where" and found "that nobody knew what," or lost his way. The cosmic fairy tale ends with the debris of ruins and souvenirs, with a very earthly archeology, not a cosmology.

****

Away from the Soviet rockets, the cosmos discovered in the girls' washroom still plays hide and seek with me. Recently I had a medical diagnosis that made me acutely aware of my mortality. A week later at the exhibit in the Boston Science Museum I saw the "Nebula Butterfly" for the first time. It was a human-scale photograph made by the engineers of the Hubble Telescope. It captures on film "the gas of a dying star that races across space at more than 600,000 miles an hour." To the flawed human eye only, it appears as a dainty and ephemeral butterfly. There is nobody else in the cosmos to admire the butterflies.

Vselennaia eschislenna I beskonechna … I smile to my teenage self and we play cat's cradle with the colorful strings of the universe. I know, I know, dear Sir George, the butterfly probably doesn't exist, just the flicker of the camera. And I? I barely exist either. "No, no, on the contrary," roams the voice with a gentle Irish accent, as if amplified by the empty glass of some three hundred years: "This cat's cradle is all yours and the butterfly is real. Real, because immaterial. You can trust it, girl. This beautiful unheroic butterfly."

2

Children, We've Been Deceived!

Once upon a time I was a brave Little Red Riding Hood. I was already four and a half; my velvet cap was bloody red and my basket was filled with the sweets of yesterday, wrapped in glittering foil.

"You were all dressed up and ready to go," my mother begins her story. "You took your stuffed giraffe with you and were not scared of the wolf. You were only afraid of doctors who gave shots. So, I told you that you were going to the show, not to the hospital. Nothing to worry about." Little Red Riding Hood was going to the House of Culture for the New Year's celebration called *yolka*. If she could sit more or less still and enjoy the show, she would get a special gift of "Bird's Milk" chocolates, named after something that doesn't exist.

At first, Little Red Riding Hood did exactly what her mom told her to, and sat more or less still. The curtain went up and a doctor wearing large glasses and a long white gown appeared on stage. His name was Dr. Aibolit, "Ay, it hurts!" "Do you remember Dr. Aibolit, the beloved hero of children's stories? He used to sing a song we all loved: 'It's actually good that we feel so bad right now!' Dr. Aibolit was carrying an injection needle, human-size. The moment you saw the needle, you jumped out of your seat and ran straight to the stage.

'Children, we've been deceived' you screamed.

'This isn't a show, this is a hospital!'

All hell broke loose. Kids began to scream and run away from their parents, following you. 'It's true, it's true!' one little boy shouted. 'Little Red Riding Hood is brave; she always tells the truth!'"

"You know this was my first year at a new job," says my mother in conclusion. "All my colleagues were there and I was so embarrassed for you. You disrupted the whole celebration."

My mom's tale of Little Red Riding Hood's feats always gave me a good feeling. I got the children out of the boring New Year's show and stood up to Dr. Aibolit: "It's not 'even good' that we are doing badly, doctor! Ay, it hurts, and it can only get worse! And why are your spectacles so big? And your needle so sharp? Hey, kids, let's get out of this silly show, grab 'Bird's Milk' without permission and run outside to play spies."

I disrupted the fairy tale because I truly believed in it. Not the way grown-ups did. They just use fairy tales to make us do something unpleasant in so-called real life: "And then Ivan the Fool went into the dark forest and stopped at the crossroads. No, he doesn't have to kill the dragon, he has a more difficult task: to go to nobody-knows-where and find nobody-knows-what …"

"And at that moment you would open your mouth very wide," my mother says laughing, "so that we could finally stuff some food into you." The food didn't taste good, some eggplant salad or codfish oil. My mom lived through hunger and was very worried that I was a poor eater. But this was no excuse. This trick was unfair to the fairy tale.

They were not made to deceive or pacify little disobedient children. They were great on their own—like in other countries. Fairy tales had real magic to them, not the petty pretense of the adult world. They made sense to us and we could master their rules better than those of real life.

During that celebration in the House of Culture I wasn't in the show at all. I was Little Red Riding Hood, flesh and blood. So what, that I wasn't a curly blond with vacant blue eyes like the goody-goody girl in my picture book "Tales of the Brothers Grimm." "Why are your eyes so big and black,

Little Red Riding Hood?" the kids in kindergarten used to tease me. "Why are they so dark and dirty? You have to wash them with some good soap." I wasn't going to cry to please them and to bleach my eyes with tears. I was a different-looking, dark-eyed Red Riding Hood, a character without a plot but full of energy.

In Russian fairy tales, the storyteller always makes excuses for himself. "I was there, I drank mead and beer, but it all ran down my whiskers, not a drop did I swallow." In short, there was a thing or two that he couldn't stomach. And if the storyteller is a woman of a certain age, with barely visible whiskers, her whole mouth might be smudged with the undigested remains of the fairy tale feast.

The memories of my childhood bleed into the edges of my mother's story. Something always remains unsaid or undigested. That forest road that Red Riding Hood took still haunts my dreams. It skirts a lake with muddy water and goes into the narrow corridor of a communal apartment, and then down the dark passage of an anonymous train station. It leaps in and out of fairy tales seamlessly and without a break. And there is a scrap of red cloth on the margins of the shot, and a narrow escape.

I hope to stumble onto something, to find a clue, a scene of fear and wonder and a Bird's Milk chocolate. Like Ivan the Fool, I have an assignment: to go to the crossroads of fear, abandoned by dragons and angels, and to find my way to "nobody-knows-where to get nobody-knows-what." I am on my way! And I promise I won't take any shortcuts or bring back any blond princesses. I will make sure to look elsewhere.

So why has little Red Riding Hood loomed so large in our childhood? The "girl meets wolf" story is just as old as the "girl meets boy" story. In the medieval tales of French and Italian peasants, a little girl meets a werewolf in the forest and reveals all her secrets to him. He quickly eats her grandma, puts on the grandma's clothes and then asks the girl to come to bed with him and finishes her for dessert. Scholars have spoken a lot about cannibalism, blood rituals, sun and moon cycles and menstruation. One thing is clear: the story is brutal; it doesn't spare cruelty and has no redemption. Violence is not hidden behind the scenes, it's right there in plain view. The modern cult of childhood hadn't been invented yet, and little peasant children were brought up on fearful tales without any palliatives.

The seventeenth-century French writer and courtier Charles Perrault created a more literary version of the story for the court of Louis IV: the girl acquires her fashionable red cape and the wolf learns gallantry. He becomes less brutal, but no less dangerous, Don Juan, the seducer. The age of the heroine stretches from childhood to early puberty; the French Red Riding Hood is a kind of Lolita in the making.

The celebrated folk tale collections of German authors, the Brothers Grimm, contained many versions, always with a virtuous blond heroine. In the later version, the little girl and her grandma outwit the wolf, because they have already read the fairy tale; they lure the beast to the house with the smell of homemade sausage and trap him fearlessly.

The Brothers Grimm were beloved by Russian and Soviet children, but after the revolution there emerged a very strong local tradition as well. Children's literature in the Soviet Union became a retreat for many experimental writers and artists who otherwise couldn't publish their work. So, without knowing it, we grew up on Aesopian tales of dissent, but also on literature that had a great sense of humor and play. Kornei Chukovsky, a poet and a friend of many great poets from Khlebnikov to Mandelshtam, was the first author of the poem about Doctor Aibolit, a kind doctor who receives a message from the monkey Chichi to go to the banks of the river Limpopo in Africa to cure Chichi's sick sisters and brothers. In 1966, a well-known film for children and adults was made called *Aibolit 66* which used shifting screens, mime, live actors and animation, and was at the forefront of cinematic experimentation. Doctor Aibolit was no superhero; he was just a great animal lover and a believer in random kindness and medical science.

In the Khrushchev era of de-Stalinization and thaw, the story of fear and seduction got another twist as an experimental cartoon, released in 1959, "Peter and Little Red Riding Hood." The Soviet pioneer Peter; a brave and mischievous boy comes late to the movie theater; the cartoon of the fairy tale "Little Red Riding Hood" had already started. Peter decides to sneak into the movie theater through the hole in the fence and suddenly finds himself right in the middle of the movie itself.

Peter has read the fairy tale and he wants to warn the blond foreign Red Riding Hood to be cautious. His true antagonist is not really the wolf but the cartoon storyteller himself. At the very beginning, Peter meets two animated announcers-narrators who guide everyone through the story. "Who are they?" Peter asks the local talking duck. "They are announcers" (*dictors*, in Russian, which sounds almost like "dictators"), they tell everybody, what everybody already knows. These dictors-dictators try to expel Petya from the cartoon; he didn't go through the vetting process! He comes uncensored! Peter so offends one of the dictors he demonstratively disconnects himself. So, while the little foreign Red Riding Hood is still a damsel in distress, she finds a new helper. The Soviet pioneer of the 1960s doesn't want to be a superhero but an author of a new kind of story.

Of course, there is no violent content in the movie. It is gentle and fun. When Soviet immigrants came to the US before perestroika, they were shocked by the violence in American popular culture. American suburban kids often saw more violence on-screen than off, and they became anaesthetized to it. By contrast, Soviet kids witnessed physical fights, alcoholism, bullying, but it was rarely represented in the movies or on television. Violence in the Soviet media was mostly off-screen, and it was rarely spoken about or recalled.

The wolf in "Petya and Red Riding Hood" is not to be feared but to be laughed at. He is just a grey wolf next door. The figure of the enemy in the 1960s is discredited and ridiculed. The whole culture of fear of the Stalin era is called into question. The new merry era of the 1960s is forward-looking, the past is mostly off-screen. And yet little children are still haunted by inexplicable fairy tales.

Let's go back to that House of Culture in Leningrad, to the cheerful Soviet 1960s of my childhood. "Thank you, dear Motherland, for a happy childhood" was the slogan. We didn't just read old tales; we were learning to draw the rockets and sputniks of the future with colored pencils. We were told that when we grow up, we would live with Communism, or at least in the Cosmos on Mars, the red planet. The melancholic Moon was for bourgeois Americans. "*C'est si bon*," "it's so good" was a popular French song of the time, sung by Yves Montand in a black turtleneck. He came to the USSR in the late 1950s and returned to France disillusioned. But never mind: his poem rhymed nicely with the Soviet phrase: "Life has become merrier, life has become better," just with a different accent.

This brief time of transition between Stalin and Brezhnev was called "the Thaw" (*ottepel'*). Some hoped it would become a Leningrad Spring, just like the later Prague Spring, but instead, the melting ice of the Soviet puddles froze over again during the Brezhnev era of stagnation (*zastoi*). But this happened later. In the early 1960s my parents were very young and hopeful. Only in their early twenties, they still wanted to catch up on everything they had missed in their own wartime childhood. Now the Great Patriotic War was over, Stalin was dead, political thaw was in and so were miniskirts and updos; new poetry readings were taking place in stadiums, and Italian movies with cat-eyed beauties and free-spirited long takes captivated audiences. Love was in the air with lyrical whispers of the new sincerity and occasional melancholic notes of 1930s tangos. "Please add that we had no shower in our communal bathroom, no toilet paper, no privacy," says my mother. "We were humiliated all the time in our everyday life. Always check with me when you write these things." Ok, done. Right after I was born, my mother and father finally got a room of their own with high ceilings in a communal apartment with the family of neighbors who were complete strangers to them. Our windows looked out onto a dark, enclosed Leningrad courtyard, but my mother bought very modern curtains in Estonia that looked like fish nets capable of capturing sea monsters and stars. As I peeped through these curtains into the dark windows and ruined balconies on the other side of the building, the world appeared to me more magical than depressing. Our room was brightly illuminated by a red lampshade made in Yugoslavia or Czechoslovakia; it looked like a friendly UFO or a gift from outer space.

When my father washed dishes in the communal kitchen, he used to sing a cheerful song: "We were born to make fairy tales come true." The song was called the "March of the Aviators" or "March of the Enthusiasts" and it had an uncanny history far from its original creators, two Jewish musicians. The song was beloved by both Nazi and Stalin propaganda. The words in the Soviet version went like this:

We were born to make fairytales come true
To conquer distances and space
We were given steel arms as wings
A flaming motor for a heart

If we look closely at the words of the song, we realize that the cheerful humanoid airplanes are not so safe for flying. To have a flame in one's heart is necessary for revolutionary enthusiasm, but when it comes to the heart of the airplane, the motor is not advised to be in flames. Mixed metaphors are unsafe. How come millions of Soviet people had been singing the song since the 1930s and nobody ever noticed the internal sabotage? This was precisely because all those millions sang it together. This Soviet fairy tale was meant to be recited by an enthusiastic marching crowd, and not read closely on a solitary page. To tell the truth, when my father sang it alone in our communal kitchen, he was happy that the Stalinist times, when the song was written, were over, and he could now laugh along with the song. The last thing we wanted was to make fairy tales come true. Let fairy tales be fairy tales. If they were to come true, the flaming motor of someone's heart would definitely explode and the collective organism would cease to function properly!

My mother would never sing a song like that. She distrusted fairy tales of any kind and hoped to instill in me a sense of reality. She was only six when Hitler's armies invaded the Soviet Union, and she had to flee to Siberia with her mother and brother. She didn't talk about it much, and I learned all the details of her wartime childhood when I was filling out her application for aid from the German government two years ago. She was approaching the application form as if it were the diary that she never kept. Her diary. I include here some of her memories that didn't fit into the application form slots. As Leningrad was under siege by the Nazi army, families with children were being evacuated. My mother, aged six, and her brother, aged nine, were separated from their mother and transported in jam-packed trains under constant bombardment to Yaroslavl, but the German armies were approaching that city too; so they fled on a swarming and overcrowded steamboat filled with screaming people to Saratov, where they reunited with their mother and their cousins and fled further to Siberia. (CUT? *There was no information in the Soviet media about Nazi executions of the Jews. After Hitler's invasion of Poland in 1939, during the Molotov–Ribbentrop pact between Stalin and Hitler, all information about the targeted extermination of the Jews was considered "propaganda," and some Polish Jews who fled to supposed safety in the Soviet Union before 1941 were arrested and ended up in the Gulag. My great-grandmother was in a hospital in Belarus as the German armies were advancing. She still had good memories from World War One, when German soldiers were much less cruel to the Jews than the local Belarusians and Ukrainians. This time she was executed. Her daughter, my grandfather's sister and her family joined my mom and her brother.*) My mom was the youngest among the children: her older cousin, a spoiled, blue-eyed Marochka, and my mom's older brother who occasionally bullied her. They all lived surrounded by the Siberian forests where non-fairy tale wolves howled gruesome lullabies. "The snow came up to the windowsills and sometimes to the floor of our rooms. I still have frostbite on my hands," says my mother. The locals were not always kind to the Jewish refugees from Leningrad. When my mother started school, the local boys followed her with a song: "kike, kike, kike, running on a little spike." It rhymes in Russian: "*zhid, zhid, zhid, po verevochke bezhit.*"

Once upon a time my mom's mother, Grandma Rosa, had to leave the children behind and make a long walk through the Siberian forest in order to reach the neighboring town. She had to sell most of their personal belongings in order to buy food for the children. While she was away and the kids were home alone, a local man stopped by their apartment. He said that Rosa was lost in the forest and she had no food left with her and was very hungry. He asked the kids to send some food. My mom and her brother Misha gave the man all the food they could find in the house. Grandma Rosa came back to the empty house. She never met that man in the forest and he vanished with all their winter reserve. This was Red Riding Hood redux, made for the dark Siberian night, without good costumes. The man was no wolf and he didn't eat little children. He just left them starving.

"I don't remember myself smiling till the age of 11. When the war was over, I began to smile and laugh again," wrote my mother in her application. I was editing her text with a pragmatic Western approach, making sure she puts the right information into the right box. "Do you really want to say this that you didn't smile till the age of eleven? You know they are looking for facts, you should say exactly in which towns you were, how you were fleeing by train and boat under German bombardment, how you lived your life with Siberian frostbite, and how traumatic it all was." "Why do you always try to embellish things?" asked my mother. "Just put it the way it happened."

My mother was most happy when she observed something beautiful and new and it didn't come from books. Books were naïve deceptions. Children, don't be deceived, life is scarier than fairy tales. Swimming was her way to joy—she feels free on the surface of the water, moving away from the shore towards the horizon, where she could escape from all the dark forests of her life, and from us too. It was my mother who taught me to swim. We still swim together, but I am much less brave than she is. Usually I don't go too far from the shore and always make sure that my feet can find the bottom. She still swims much better than me. I come out and read in the shade, observing my mother at a distance in the middle of the lake. "Life is not literature," my mother tells me with mild reproach. Of course, I am a literature professor and somehow it ended up being my life.

For my father, the difference between life and books or films was never so crucial. What was important was shared experience, a sincere intonation, the right mood. In this sense, he was very 1960s. He was ten during the war: his father stayed in Leningrad during the blockade, while his mother, my grandmother Sonia, was arrested and spent six years in the Gulag. As a teenager during the war, he grew up believing that there exist "us" and "them," true friends and real enemies, and the most important and difficult thing is to distinguish one from the other. Perhaps not finding such clear demarcations in his everyday life, my father loved to organize imagined communities, clubs, states within the state, playing games with other childish adults. First, he organized the Club of Faithful Fans of Zenit (KZBZ in Russian), dedicated to the Leningrad football team that lost the game on the day I was born. Then my father created his labor of love, the movie club "Kino and You," in the Petrograd District House of Culture on Leo Tolstoy Square, near our home. This wasn't a place merely to see movies that weren't shown in official Soviet theaters, it was more of a pretext to talk about life, to create a true community of friends and film club members. My father's club was like a little 1960s fairy tale kingdom with kinder laws, a little more freedom of speech. There was a lot of talk there, not much action and a lot of dreaming. The film club was my unofficial babysitting station. I was brought there from an early age. When I was a child, my father sometimes read me fairy tales and petted me on the head as if I were a little fairy tale animal. He even called me *zver'*, a little beast, and told me not to be afraid.

My parents started leaving me alone from the age of five. They didn't go too far, just across the square to my father's film club in the local Palace of Culture, to play their own adult games. Italian neo-realist films, black-and-white and tantalizingly open-ended, were followed by intense Polish existential dramas and French comedies. The club "Kino and You" was not only a place to watch movies, but also to talk about them, to see and to be seen. Since some of the movies had more adult content than a five-year old could take, I was left in our room in the communal apartment with the drunken neighbors. Though in the US leaving little children alone would be considered unthinkable, in the Soviet Union of my childhood this was the norm. Strangely, I retain good memories of this time spent alone, when I somehow created my own time-space of fun and freedom—with flashes of fear. My mother tells me that I was a very well-behaved girl then. She or my dad would set the alarm clock to 9:30, and at that time I had to go straight to bed and not wait for them to come home. Sometimes, they would find me in bed asleep in my dress and even an apron, because I was so obedient and tried to go to sleep on time. Parents, you've been deceived. Of course, I didn't follow orders. I would play as long as I wished and then once I heard their footsteps on the staircase, I would jump into bed and pretend to be sleeping, just like the wolf in grandma's clothes.

My grandmother Sonia disapproved of my parents leaving me alone in our communal flat. She would call me and start asking me questions:

"Did you check under the bed, Svetochka? Bend your knees and look underneath? Maybe there is a wicked thief hiding there? Did you check the back door? Are the big hook and the chain on? Did you check behind the fishnet curtains in the dark corner?" Luckily there was only one-and-a-half rooms, so there wasn't much space for the wicked thief to hide. My grandma was a Gulag survivor. She had nightmares about being arrested again. Unwittingly I inherited some of them.

Other than looking for wicked thieves under the bed, I found these breaks from my dear parents fun. Books kept me company. I discovered that there are many more things one could do with them than with my favorite stuffed giraffe or that East German rubber doll Nelly, with her bleached-blond hair and glass eyes. Once I twisted off the doll's head to see what was inside it. There was nothing there, just the emptiness of pink rubber. Books smelled much better—a mixture of Soviet printing glue and unforeseen adventure.

Once upon a time when I was five and a half, my parents came back from the film club and entered a new fairy tale. They discovered that instead of reading the book that they left for me, I had begun to write a book of my own. My heroes were mostly red vegetables—Signorina Carrot and Signore Pomodoro (courtesy of the Italian communist writer Gianni Rodari). Who did what to whom? I don't remember. One more realistic story featured a little girl who went to play on a slide in the park shaped like sputniks. The girls didn't fly into the Cosmos but just slid down the slippery slope. (I am embellishing, as usual. My early stories began and ended in *media res* and had poor character development.)

I didn't put my name on the cover of my first book, although I already knew how to spell it. Instead I wrote in big letters, TALES OF THE BROTHERS GRIMM. I thought that was the only book worth contributing to, like a book of life. One shared collection of fairy tales with many slippery slopes and curvy paths, scared Gretchens and wise Vassilissas. Thus, Little Red Riding Hood became a little sister Grimm.

This sister-writer was the perfect babysitter. Writing protected me from the wicked thief or the drunk neighbor urinating in the corridor. I didn't need a large number of toys that would become quickly obsolete and abandoned. Nor did I depend on the digital screen, that would spoil me with instant gratification under my fingertips, courtesy of software engineers and advertisers. VRI, Virtual Reality of the Imagination, was the only available Soviet app, free with the purchase of colored pencils.

Literature became my best imaginary friend. Not just a specific literary character, but literature as such offered an entry into another world created through language and pictures, an alternative space out of space and time out of time. The empty white pages at the end of the book were my favorite. I could draw there and practice letters *in cursive*. Literature was the best game that I could play alone, or rather with all kinds of creatures dead and alive, realistic and fantastic, from the Black Forest of Little Red Riding Hood to the Limpopo river of Dr. Aibolit.

Literature also provided the best romance, at least till I was a teenager. I just couldn't have crushes on the little sweaty boys with pimples from the 6-B class. Instead, I created imaginary Prince Charmings for myself, and even wrote secret messages from them to me which I would demonstratively "leave behind" in front of the boys from 6-B. He had a foreign fairy-tale name, Dmitri Brunie: Karamazov meets D'Artagnan.

When I was in the sixth grade, I took part in the literary Olympiad, where we had to write a composition on the topic "My favorite hero." The stock of preferred heroes included young Lenin dreaming of the Bolshevik party, Pavlik Morozov from the 1930s (who informed on his father for the sake of the motherland) and Vasek Trubachev, who did something equally positive. My choice of the musketeer D'Artagnan cost me my prize. I received an honorable mention and a quiet reprimand for choosing a foreign hero. Was D'Artagnan, with his dark and thick moustache, a suave wolf in musketeer's clothing? Even my father began to worry about my passion for D'Artagnan, and with my mother's encouragement he decided to talk to me and to turn me away from that dark, handsome and reckless man, who in any case, "was emotionally (and physically) unavailable."

"Did you know that D'Artagnan never brushed his teeth?" asked my father in a conspiratorial tone. "He must have really smelled. Do you see any mention of D'Artagnan brushing his teeth in the book?"

He was right. There was no mention. I was shocked. The taste of D'Artagnan's sour breath kept me up at night. It almost destroyed my faith in tall, dark and handsome men from the Old World. I remember that when I came to America, one of the first things we were taught in our new immigrant orientation program was to brush our teeth regularly and to use deodorant and contraceptives. The rumor about Soviet bad teeth must have spread westwards. We had to bring our oral hygiene up to the standards of the New World. After thirty years in America I can testify that people here have fresher breath than in the old country, but my brave hero-friend, the faithful musketeer, is missing. Gone flossing?

Once upon a time I met a Leningrad D'Artagnan. It took place in a half-empty trolley No. 1, which I regularly took from school back home. I might have been ten or eleven. He was standing next to my seat and leaning against me as the trolley bus went along its bumpy route. My D'Artagnan was in his late twenties and had dark hair and kind dark eyes. He looked like a member of my father's film club or an extra in one of the second-rate Italian movies that they showed there. I was reading dialogues in my English textbook. He tried to strike up a conversation, but I didn't answer. I had been taught not to talk to strangers. When he saw that I was doing English dialogues he asked me in English: "What is your name?" "My name is Sveta," I answered like a good pupil. We had an intelligent small conversation in Russian. And then he asked me where I was going and where I lived. I wasn't in the forest but in public transportation, and I wasn't carrying a cabbage pie to my grandmother, but just coming home to an empty apartment in a dark enclosed courtyard. He got off the trolley with me. We walked silently for a while.

"Can I come with you and help you with your homework?" he asked.

"No thank you," I said politely. "My mother told me not to talk to strangers."

I lingered at the trolley stop because I already knew that a good spy has to cover her traces and mislead. The stranger didn't insist. He looked sad, his eyes were dark and kind. "Goodbye," he said and walked slowly towards the buildings of the Medical Institute nearby. I have no idea whether this was an act of random kindness or of random pedophilia. I only got scared afterwards.

"Why did you talk to him in the first place?" my mother asked. "Didn't I tell you to never talk to strangers?" "But he looked like somebody from the film club," I said.

There are two approaches to fear. The American way: there is nothing to fear but fear itself. Confront the fear, head-on, like one cowboy confronting the other: a fair fight, a few broken ribs and you'll be the toast of the tavern. In Russia you don't talk about fear. You don't run to the stage and scream "wolf!" You turn your back on fear, recklessly or cautiously, depending on the situation. In his autobiographical novella *The Egyptian Stamp*, poet Osip Mandelshtam wrote something that goes against the grain of both traditions: "With fear I have no fear." Figure out the cause of your fear, give it space, make architecture for it. Imagine the fear as a nomadic home and carry it through your story. "Fear takes me by the hand and leads my way," writes Mandelshtam at the end of his tale, moving from the third person to the first.

Literature was both a source of fear and a cure for it; it distracted us from the world around us, but also provided an alternative guide to life. Unlike ideology, it taught us to tolerate ambiguity, to explore the world of possibility and wonder, to cross borders into foreign times and spaces that were otherwise beyond reach.

During my teenage years, my games were no longer solitary. My comrade-in-arms in our early teenage years was my best friend, Natasha-Kycha; we were like two musketeers, one for all and all for one. Our games were rituals for an imaginary community of friends. One such game was called the game of secrets. The "secret" was a rescued piece of trash, a glittering foil wrapping of already-eaten chocolates, a piece of colored glass, a shard of bone china with gilded edges and blue flowers. The game consisted in burying this precious treasure from the trash somewhere on the outskirts of a public place, by the fence of the garden or behind some shrubbery. The secrets were hidden in order to be shared with a special few. Intimacy wasn't based on total exposure but on intimation, not on over-sharing but on understanding one another with half-words. Visiting the secret burial place was a ritual of friendship. All children's games were, one way or another, games of hide and seek, of intimation and cover-up. They carved out uncharted territories for kids that existed in a different scale and invisibly for grown-ups.

Our friendship was real and literary at the same time. At the age of thirteen we walked through the interconnected courtyards and discussed our melancholic and belated times, the era of Brezhnev's stagnation. We read too much Mikhail Lermontov for our classes and thought that the golden age of Pushkin (or the 1960s?) was over, and somehow the silver age was over too, and we lived in some non-descript, grey age. We learned Lermontov's short poem by heart: "I'm bored and sad and there's nobody to shake my hand. And life, if you look around and think about it, is just an empty and stupid joke." We identified with the Hero of Our Time, the enigmatic Don Giovanni named Pechorin, whose eyes didn't smile when he smiled. He was traveling aimlessly in postwar times along the Crimean shore, playing games of chance with a Serbian gambler or seducing a beautiful Circassian girl named Bela, without much pleasure.

Even our hooliganism was literary. We used to play phone tricks on strangers. For example, we would check the names in the phone book and when we would find Dostoevsky, we would call and ask politely: "Is this Dostoevsky?" "Yes, Dostoevsky speaking," responded a deep male voice. "Idiot!" we would scream in response. We were caught at our own game when we reached a Mrs. Lermontova, and tried to ask her if she was bored and sad and had nobody to shake her hand, it turned out that it was all true, and she wouldn't let us go without a long poetic conversation that we desperately tried to end.

All our books were about male friendships, but really the relationships of our early teens were all among girls. We had one small gang of former Little Red Riding Hoods pitched against another one.

When I was in the fifth grade, the class master put me on school trial. It was a mini-version of a show trial. I was accused of organizing secret societies, conspiring against other pupils in the class, and writing a slanderous novel about it. The accusation wasn't entirely untrue. Kycha and I had organized a notorious secret society of Black Mimosas, and we sent chivalrous messages to the leader of the other girls' gang, the beautiful A-student Katya P., now happily residing in Canada. I think we actually liked each other and somehow it was understood that this was only an adventurous game, like in *The Three Musketeers*. Our secret message was peppered with classical references:

Femida has been bribed. Let Fortuna help you!
Black Mimosas.

Russian Mimosas were normally the flowers that boys gave girls for International Women's Day; they were semi-dry and sickly-yellow in color, but with a tender smell. Our mimosas were ever-black but we wrote our messages in milk, just like young Lenin in his prison cell. This was the most interesting thing we learned in the long history of Leninism; how Lenin made an inkpot out of bread and poured some milk in it and began writing secret messages explaining that we, the true revolutionaries, "would take a different path." You had to bring the sheet of paper close to a flame and watch the shaking letters emerge in front of your eyes. It felt like uncovering hieroglyphs of the past.

Except for the threat that Femida, the Goddess of Justice, has been bribed, the messages weren't particularly violent. The trial wasn't initiated by Katya herself, who rather enjoyed the attention we were showering on her and was herself an excellent player. It was her divorced father, who might have felt guilty that he didn't visit his daughter very often, who informed on us to the ideologically obsessed teacher. During the trial I had to face the whole class and listen to the accusations in conspiracy with a straight face and unblinking eyes, thinking of brave D'Artagnan. Kycha was the only one who testified for me. My parents, too, were on my side, somehow; they knew it wasn't for real, but they treated the event as yet another disciplinary measure of our authoritarian class master. After the trial we ran to our headquarters in the girls' toilet where we could cry freely and support each other.

Kycha stayed behind in Leningrad when I went to pioneer camp. It might have been there, when I was fourteen, that I played my last game. Like in the old fairy tales, there was a dark forest with protruding roots and bright red mushrooms with white dots, a lovely lake with muddy waters and salty cabbage pies in the collective canteen. This was the pioneer camp affiliated with my father's factory, which had its own mini House of Culture with shows and marches. We still wore our dirty pioneer ties, but mine had a torn end. I didn't like getting up in the morning, making my bed in two minutes army-style and running to march with the other sleepy overgrown pioneers: *One, two three: Pioneers are we! We are the pioneers. Who's marching in one line—our pioneer detachment! Pioneers, to struggle for the cause of the Communist party be ready! Answer, salute: Always Ready!*

My parents knew that I had outgrown my pioneer salutes, but the camp was in such a fairy-tale natural setting, and in any case, there was nowhere else to put me up that summer. On the first day of the camp I met a girl my age, an engineer's daughter from my father's factory called Alla. She was tall, handsome and athletic, with the broad shoulders of a professional swimmer. Her dirty blond hair was tied in a neat ponytail. It was instant attraction and intense friendship. We walked, swam together and talked about books and boys, more the former than latter.

In the beginning we were enchanted by each other—by our common interests and differences. But Alla was a natural leader and I was always in the party of the opposition. We started to grow apart. She had her own fan club of girls from our detachment and they had long discussions on everything from new make-up purchased on the black market to sports and contraceptives. They had their own games of secrets, too, in which I didn't partake. Alla was the ring mistress, and I was the only one who resisted her domineering charms.

I remember girls' chatter, not-so-clean pioneer ties hanging at the heads of the narrow beds, and me hiding in my bed, my back turned to the others, escaping to the Sherwood Forest of my English book. In our English classes we always read about the people's heroes—from Robin Hood to the Angry Young Men. In our classes on English phonetics we sat in front of the mirror and were taught some mythical nineteenth-century British English that required us to open our mouths and show teeth making the uncanny grin of a Cheshire cat. I preferred Robin Hood and his coterie of ragtag friends who stole from the rich to Alla's blue-shaded, deodorant-sharing pioneers. I was neither with them nor against them—just to the side, a fellow non-traveler.

Alla couldn't tolerate this kind of defiant non-belonging. She started to refer to me as *zhidovka* (a kike in feminine) and to make anti-Semitic remarks. I didn't react because they didn't seem to have any bearing on our relationship. One girl from Alla's fan club even came up to me and said sweetly that I didn't really "look Jewish." She thought I was OK. This wasn't a struggle around prejudice but around power. Alla became conspicuously aggressive and I was studiously defiant. In the meantime, we marched together in the morning and swore pioneer friendship and participated in swimming competitions, since we were both good swimmers.

Once our pioneer leader, a man in his twenties with mild manners and a long moustache where lots of beer and tall tales traveled, selected Alla and me for a special trip to the forest lake. He used this occasion to meet his own paramour, a female cultural organizer from another detachment. Alla and I were left alone to swim in the forest lake without adult supervision.

That lake—moon-shaped with weeping willows on the banks—stayed with me. The water was eerily calm and muddy. I was swimming slowly, feeling the dark green algae under my fingers. And then my head was underwater and I couldn't see anymore. Somebody was pressing me hard face down. Holding me forcefully under water, a few seconds, a minute, an eternity. I tried to escape and come back to the surface but someone's hand kept pushing me down. There was no bottom under my feet, nothing to grasp to. I choked.

Was this only a game? The drowned and the saved?
I don't know, I had no name for it.

I can't remember how I managed to make it to the shore and somehow laugh it off. I ran to the village store near the camp and called my father. I asked him to take me out of the camp. He said that he couldn't. He realized it was tough for me, but such was life in the country, and I needed to learn to survive. He promised to move me to another detachment as quickly as he could. I don't blame him because I didn't tell him exactly what happened. I couldn't utter it, and he wouldn't have been able to hear it anyway. He didn't ask any follow-up questions. Perhaps he was afraid to have his own worst fears realized.

I wished somebody else had witnessed what happened at that lake, not just me. It could have been a lumberjack from a nearby village, a kindly Baba Yaga walking home to her hut on chicken legs, a Princess Frog or at least a talking duck who could do a good underwater shot. Maybe they could tell another version of the story with a different ending: an athletic girl kissing a scared friend on a wet cheek, a pioneer leader diving to save me, me fighting back and swimming in brave pioneer strokes back to the shore.

But the talking duck had already been eaten. The pioneer leader was necking with his girlfriend. My mother and grandmother were far away, in some house of culture. My adversary was a handsome athletic blond girl who looked like a heroine of the Socialist Realist paintings. An overgrown Little Red Riding Hood, whom everybody liked, put an end to my childhood games.

More importantly, I might have misrecognized my Prince Charming. He wasn't a suave wolf, pioneer Peter or D'Artagnan, but Doctor Aibolit with the huge needle. I should have run towards him, not away from him. Why is it that kind doctors are made unsexy in world literature? From Flaubert to Chekhov, they come out as mild-mannered and kindly cuckolds. Dr. Aibolit would have led me to a kinder world of painted lakes and singing monkeys, where small human deeds really matter and there is still a place for artistic play and random kindness. When I watch *Aibolit 66* today—the 1966 film made for both children and adults—I realize once again there was no single female character there with whom I could identify. Even the singing monkey Chichi, the doctor's friend, was a perky blond.

My mother tells me the story one more time of my protest at the House of Culture. She describes how hard she tried to make a good costume for me with the help of Aunt Genia, who was an excellent tailor, and how I embarrassed her at the end, for no reason. Dr. Aibolit was just about to sing his song about how it's actually good that things are pretty bad, or how we should all be happy whether we like it or not.

"'Children, we were deceived,' you screamed, and all the kids ran after you."

"I wish I could do it again," I said. "Just go out there and shout what I mean. I was so brave then."

"You were very scared," said my mother.

3

The Secret Life of a Communal Apartment Neighbor

Till the age of seven I lived in the same room with my parents. The first memory that comes to my mind is that of the heavy curtain (*port'era*) that partitioned our shared room. Dark yellow, with heavy ornamental appliqué, the portiere was a porous partition between children and adults. During my parents' parties—*vecherinki*—the portiere took human shapes as the guests walked in and out of the child's corner. Smudged silver shades, blurry cat-eyes, unfolding updos, young sweat on the polyester dresses and the inevitable "tape recorder music" in the background with its adventurous unofficial ease. It might have been my favorite song by Vladimir Vysotsky. Then I thought it was about funny baobabs. Actually, it was about migrating souls.

> *Some people trust Muhammad, and some- Jesus for salvation,*
> *And there are also such types who treat these ones with spite,*
> *While there is Hindus' idea of the soul's transmigration,*
> *Which says that we don't die for good, and I believe it's right.*
> *Enjoy your life and don't be cross,*
> *Don't gripe about your fate –*
> *Directly into a big boss*

Your soul may migrate.
Don't worry if ye're but a hand, ye'll be reborn a foreman,
With time ye'll be a minister – it's really not a joke!
If you act dumb – too bad for you, then for some thousand years
you'll be reborn a baobab and die a baobab.[1]

I didn't know what religion meant; for me the song was the greatest fairy tale. Nobody died. Everyone traveled elsewhere and became somebody or something else. I wanted to become a babbling baobab and dance all night with the youthful grown-ups.

My life unfolded around partitions, doors, walls and curtains of many kinds—from the porous portiere in the room of my parents to the invisible but perceivable iron curtain. There was always a place for a shadow play and a desire for secrecy in the midst of collective exposure. For as long as I can remember, I always hoped to transmigrate—if not into a big boss, at least into an exotic plant or bird with a foreign afterlife. Like the majority of urban kids of my generation, I was a single child; this was partly due to the difficult housing arrangements in the communal apartments. The Soviet single child was treated as a part of a larger group, a member of unofficial and official collectives—not just a nuclear family. My first childhood memories are public, not intimate. I am in the company of my parents' friends and members of the extended family, like my perky cousins with whom I had little in common. My parents have an exceptional record—a loving marriage of half a century, yet I didn't spy on their intimacy. Most of all, I remember the texture of our partition. So much for the primal scenes and Victorian Peeping Toms.

The partition was the central architectural feature of Soviet communal living. Some were mere curtains but most of them were made of plywood and they marked the intersection of public and private spheres within the apartment. After the expropriation and nationalization of property, especially

---

[1] Vladimir Vysotsky, "Pesenka o pereselenii dush" ("Song of the Soul's Transmigration").

in residential blocks in the old city center, the rooms and hallways were partitioned and subdivided, creating weird angular spaces, with a window opening onto a sunless back yard or without any windows. Every tenant exercised their imagination in inventing curtains and screens to delineate their minimum privacy. A plywood partition was so much flimsier than a wall, more a sign of division than division itself. It let through all the noises, the snoring, the fragments of conversations, the footsteps of the neighbor, and everything else you can think of. The partition served not so much to preserve intimacy as to create an illusion that some intimacy was possible.

Secrecy is one of the most important ways of keeping the illusion of privacy. But secrecy in the communal apartment was a game of searching for alternative communalities. There used to be an unofficial children's game we played in the kindergarten, called "the game of burying secrets" which had nothing to do with the official collective "hide-and-seek" orchestrated by the teacher, a game in which there were no secrets and nothing in particular to seek or to find. Our game consisted of a ritual burial of our little "secret" somewhere on the outskirts of a small urban garden or yard where the teachers brought us. The secret was not precious in itself: a piece of colored glass found in the trash; an old stamp; a piece of the glittering foil wrapping of chocolates; an old badge. The burial ceremony was performed by a group of close friends and hidden from the kindergarten authorities. The secret had to be hidden in order to be shared, to become a bond between friends, a talisman of our hidden community. This secrecy is not solitary; it has to be dramatized in public. Games of secrets were played by adults in their attempts to establish alternative communities and styles of personal collecting, which was not the same as individual privacy. The space of the communal apartment defined the topography of my childhood nightmares and dreams. Maybe if I manage to reconstruct it, I can find a secret burrow to my younger self? To the Svetka, Zenita carving her little corner for private games.

Here is another scene that lays bare the boundaries between public and private in the communal apartment. The same song is playing about baobabs but this time it's not for dancing but warding off the curious neighbors and keeping the conversation more private.

My parents are having foreign guests for the first time in their life in our room in the communal apartment. Our neighbors, Aunt Vera and Uncle Fedia, are home. (Russian children call their neighbors aunt and uncle, as if they were members of one very extended family.) Uncle Fedia usually came home drunk, and if Aunt Vera refused to let him in, he would crash right in the middle of the long corridor, the central thoroughfare of the communal apartment, obstructing the entrance to our room. As a child, I would often play with peacefully reclining and heavily intoxicated Uncle Fedia, with his fingers and buttons, or tell him a story to which he probably did not have much to add. This time we were all in the room, listening to music to tone down the communal noises, and my mother was telling our foreign guests about the beauties of Leningrad: "you absolutely must go to the Hermitage, and then to Pushkin's apartment museum, and of course to the Russian Museum." In the middle of the conversation, as the guest was commenting on the riches of Russian culture, a little yellow stream slowly made its way through the door of the room. Smelly, embarrassing, intrusive, it formed a little puddle right in front of the dinner table.

No one seems to remember what happened afterwards. In the apartment, Uncle Fedia and Aunt Vera were displaced by lonely Aunt Valia, who worked in a bread factory, and her mentally ill son Yura, and then by a couple of homonymic drunkards, Aunt Shura and Uncle Shura, who endearingly called themselves the "Shurenkis." And if it were not for the benevolent foreign guest enjoying the beauties of Soviet public places, and for my mother's deeply personal embarrassment, the story would not have been particularly exceptional. After all, as one of my Soviet friends remarked, some neighbors peed into each other's teapots. Yet this scene, with its precarious coziness of a family gathering, both intimate and public, with a mixture of ease and fear in the presence of foreigners and neighbors, remained in my mind as a memory of home. The family picture is thus framed by the inescapable stream of Uncle Fedia's urine, which so easily crossed the minimal boundaries of our communal privacy, embarrassing the fragile etiquette of communal propriety. And it smells too much to turn it into a mere metaphor. This is something that is hard to domesticate.

If there had been such a thing as a Soviet cultural unconscious, it would have been structured like a communal apartment with flimsy partitions between public and private, between control and intoxication. The Soviet "family romance" was adulterated by the fluttering sound of a curious neighbor's slippers in the communal apartment, or by an inquisitive representative of the local Housing Committee. It was a romance with the collective, unfaithful to both communitarian mythologies and traditional family values.

The communal apartment was the cornerstone of Soviet civilization. It was a specifically Soviet form of urban living, a memory of a never implemented utopian communist design, an institution of social control, and the breeding ground of police informants between the 1920s and the 1980s. This is a place where many battles for the reconstruction of daily life were launched and most of them were lost. Here the neighbors engaged in quite un-Marxist class struggles; "domestic trash" triumphed and privacy was prohibited only to be reinvented again against all odds. *Kommunalka*—a term of endearment and deprecation—came into existence after the post-revolutionary expropriation and resettlement of the private apartments in urban centers. It consisted of all-purpose rooms (living rooms, bedrooms, and studies became a "decadent luxury") integrated with "places of communal use," a euphemistic expression for shared bathroom, corridor, and kitchen, spaces where hung schedules of communal duties and where endless complaints were exchanged among the fellow neighbors. The communal neighbors, most often complete strangers from different classes and social groups thrown together by the local Housing

Committee, were joined in a pre-modern practice of "mutual responsibility." (Every communal apartment dweller is probably scarred for life by that symbolic "mutual responsibility"—a double bind of love and hatred, of envy and attachment, of secrecy and exhibitionism, of embarrassment and compromise.) The communal apartment was not merely an outcome of the post-revolutionary housing crisis but also of a revolutionary experiment in living, an attempt to practice utopian ideologies and to destroy bourgeois banality. Hence this is a Soviet common place par excellence, which reveals all the paradoxes of the common place and of Soviet communality. The archeology of the communal apartment reveals what happens when utopian designs are put into practice, inhabited, and placed into history—individual and collective.

It also stands as a metaphor of the distinctive Soviet mentality. It was a favorite tragicomic setting for jokes. Thus, when Stalin was taken out of the mausoleum, people joked that Khrushchev had resettled Lenin's communal apartment (which in the post-Soviet time might be further privatized). Actually, this joke is appropriate since the communal apartment was conceived in Lenin's head. Only a few weeks after the October Revolution of 1917 Lenin drafted a plan to expropriate and resettle private apartments. This plan inspired many architectural projects of communal housing and new revolutionary topography. The "rich apartment" was defined by Lenin "as the apartment where the number of rooms equals or surpasses the number of residents who permanently inhabit this apartment." A minimum living space of about ten square meters per person and thirteen square meters per family was established. In his memoirs Joseph Brodsky calls his family's living quarters, poetically and quite literally, "a room and a half." What appears striking in Lenin's decree is that it suggests a different understanding of home and space than one is used to in Western Europe or in the United States. A person, or rather a statistical unit (in Lenin's expression, the soul of the population), was not entitled to a room or to a private space but only to a number of square meters. The space is divided mathematically or bureaucratically as if it were an abstract problem in geometry, not the real space of existing apartments. As a result, most of the apartments in the major cities were partitioned in an incredible and often non-functional manner, creating strange spaces, long corridors, and so-called "black entrances" through labyrinthine inner courtyards.

Imagine entering one of the communal apartments in Leningrad/St. Petersburg, not mine but the one across the street. We pass by the back staircase and stop in front of the massive door with several separate bells: "three rings for Petrov, two for Khaimovich, one for Skripkina, four for Genalidze." This is the first affirmation of separateness; if we don't have a separate door, at least we've got a separate doorbell; if not a separate kitchen, at least a separate gas burner. If we share the same electric light, then each of us should have a switch; even if it is completely irrational and inconvenient, we will go all the way along the long corridor to our room in order to turn on the lights in the toilet. In circumstances of extreme over-crowdedness and imposed collectivity there is an extreme almost obsessive protection of minimal individual property. Just be sure to remember how many times you have to ring the bell, and God forbid you ring the wrong one! As you enter the communal corridor you hear the flutter of slippers and the squeaking of the floors and you notice many pairs of eyes scrutinizing you through half-opened doors. Some look at you indifferently, others with suspicion or with basic self-defensive hostility, just in case. When a guest comes to the apartment it is everyone's business, a mini-event, a source of gossip and argument. Please don't forget to clean your feet, right on the threshold of the communal apartment. Do it thoroughly and just a bit longer than needed, otherwise you will violate the schedule of communal duties, especially the timetable of corridor-cleaning, and bring a lot of communal misfortune to your host.

A never-composed oral history of a Soviet communal apartment, where KGB informants and Gulag survivors, kitchen dissidents and drunks shared the same toilet and read the same newspaper *Pravda* there, offers an alternative oral history of the whole country. My grandmother Rosa lived with ten families in the partitioned apartment of the lawyer Goldberg (not a relative) who was resettled into one room and died during the Leningrad blockade. The collective included an old woman named Glebovna, who claimed to have swept the floors of the Winter Palace, and had been a maid of the first owner of the apartment (she hid a little photograph of Tsar Nikolai II in the back of a drawer); Gertruda Genrikovna, a piano teacher of German descent, who was exiled during the war to a special camp for Russified Germans in Kazakhstan and had nineteenth-century porcelain figurines representing all the nations of Great Russia; there was the former Stakhanovite and now drunkard Uncle Kolia; an old Bolshevik, Aunt Aleftina who worked as an accountant in Smolny and later for the Leningrad Party Committee and used to enjoy special vacations in the Party sanatorium. In the 1950s, during the purges of Jewish doctors, Aleftina stopped talking with my grandmother in the communal kitchen, checking if she was using any blood in her sauce. Luckily in the later post-Stalinist years their kitchen was guarded by a handsome and mostly semi-naked sailor Nikita, a KGB informant of a younger generation. He displayed the special Peruvian panties he bought for his perpetual fiancé Galya, who when Nikita went sailing befriended Leningrad underground poets.

The communal apartment is not to be confused with a kibbutz or merely an apartment with roommates. There were many utopian projects of garden cities and houseboats with common kitchens and collectivized children. Some of these avant-garde buildings are now beautiful ruins of unfulfilled modernity. Communal apartments might have shared some tenets with these architectural dreams but were mostly arbitrarily remodeled and unfairly distributed old city apartments. Since the late 1920s and especially during the Stalin years the communal apartment had become a major Soviet institution of social control and a form of constant surveillance that lasted until perestroika.

Alone, in the communal apartment, 1964–1975

Twenty years ago, I thought that if I transform myself from an unhappy communal apartment dweller into a cheerful scholarly mythologist of Soviet life, I would be able to recreate the Soviet common places. Looking back at my textual communal apartment I see many spaces of forgetting. What I forgot or didn't feel was worthy of writing were more individual experiences in the collectivized space, in particular, my own.

Being alone as a child in the communal apartment seems like a paradox, yet that's what stayed most in my memory. I look at my childhood pictures and notice my unsmiling face, except for a perky look with a fake dimple on the retouched picture taken in the official photo-atelier where I am dressed like Little Red Riding Hood. I seem to have more of a relationship with my giraffe than with my same-age cousins with bigger ribbons in their cute girlish hair. I believe my childhood was a pretty good one, considering the circumstances, but somehow in my first childhood memories I pretended to be childish. I remember less of being a child and more about trying to "pass for a child" and later longing to be a child when I was one no more.

From the age of five, my parents left me alone in our room in the communal apartment to go the film club "Kino and You" which was located in the Palace of Culture on Leo Tolstoy Square. I wasn't particularly unhappy about that at all, more curious. I was supposed to go to bed according to the alarm clock at 9:30. I rather loved my time alone. I had my parents' large room all for myself and felt like a princess in disguise. I drew pictures, I didn't have to clean my drawers or pretend to play with silly rubber German dolls. I could draw pictures and letters. Occasionally my grandmother would call and inquire if I had checked under the bed for a wicked thief or if the crook on the back door was properly in place. "You were such an obedient girl then," my mom usually says with a wistful sigh. "You always went to bed exactly according to the alarm clock. You tried so hard to be on time, that you would hide under the blanket in your half-unbuttoned dress and close your eyes." Yeah, right. I had to disappoint my mother about many things. I wasn't a virgin when I married my first husband. And no, I didn't go to sleep on the sound of the alarm clock. I jumped into bed with my dress still on when I heard my parents' footsteps on our back staircase. And I didn't keep my eyes wide shut.

On one of many such nights out, my parents came back to my half-asleep self and discovered a little notebook on the floor. On the cover, written in shaky colored letters in my five-year-old handwriting was "Tales of the Brothers Grimm." Inside they found my stories in big letters in colored pencils. The stories (written by me) were mostly about the red vegetables—Signorina Carrot escaping the evil grip of Signore Pommodore (courtesy of the Italian communist writer Gianny Rodari). There was also a more realistic tale about a girl who wants to go to the slides (*gorki*) in the garden shaped like a sputnik but there are evil boys there. (It remained open-ended.) The reader of fairy tales left unsupervised by the communal apartment committee became a writer! How could she watch the alarm clock when she was in the middle of going down the cosmic slide?

I thought from those early hours of solitude I learned to be creative, to inhabit my own world and just hang out with imaginary friends. Who needs parents or neighbors when you can just draw eyes on your thigh and wrap your knee with the sheet, white like a blank canvas? And then you can tell secrets to your imaginary friend. If only my grandma didn't call sharing her Gulag fears, it would be better. That wicked thief under my bed made funny noises even when I saw no trace of him. I continued looking under that bed even when my grandma wasn't calling. He haunted the dusty darkness in the closet. At least I knew that the alarm clock was lovingly set for me by my parents for 9:30 and that sooner or later they would come home after the movie and hopefully this would happen before the big cartoonish wolf would eat my dear grandmother

Sonia, put on her old secondary school teacher glasses and squash her favorite little Tchaikovsky bust on her bureau with his bestial paw.

Maybe in those moments I discovered both creativity and panic. They lived next to each other like neighborly Jekyll and Hyde. One was euphoric and the other scary. At the age of seven, in the first grade I inherited my grandmother Sonia's six-square-meter room and moved out of my parents' quarter with the floral bas-relief on the ceiling. In my newly conquered kingdom, I could dream of an ever-expanding world. I drank a lot of weak sweet tea with the bisé cookies that my grandmother Sonia made and looked through her window into the narrow yard with ruined balconies. I was close now to the kitchen and the door to the "black staircase" with dirty water in the basement that stored the childhood fears I could never face.

As a teenager, I escaped regularly to the happy underground of writing. I was no underground woman though (not as nasty and sickly as I thought Dostoevsky's character to be). Besides, my hero was the passionate and ironic poet of the "lost generation" (of the 1830s) Mikhail Lermontov. After several sequels I stopped writing "Tales of the Brothers Grimm," and just wrote sketches for a novel about a Spanish nun Dolores who had a double and a magic ring. The powers of that ring are now forgotten; I abandoned the novel since it was discovered and publicly ridiculed by our class master. I continued to write poems about the knight in shining armor who always lingers and never arrives on time. These were followed by a realistic chronicle of the girls' games in our class that culminated with the secret society "The Black Mimosas" that I started with my best friend Kycha. Our motto was inspired by not listening to our history teacher: "Femida has been bribed! Let Fortuna help us!" We were like two female musketeers—one for all and all for one. Girls' friendships are undervalued in culture, you have to go to male role models and "bromances" to use my teenage niece's favorite word. Kycha was a friend in need, the first and the most faithful.

As a teenager I discovered the space of interiority between the covers of the slim green notebooks, with Pushkin's verses about liberty on the front cover and multiplication tables on the back, made by the Leningrad factory "Svetoch" with the "Order of the Red Banner of Labor." The diary writing lasted from 1974 till my immigration when I had to leave the skinny green notebooks behind in the Soviet Union due to the limit and potential subversive quality of the "hand written documents" that were subject to strict inspection. It's hard for me to imagine what the custom's officer would have made of Lermontov's angst and my teenage angst repeated throughout the notebooks: "And life, if surveyed with cold-blooded regard, is stupid and empty – a joke …"

Here are some excerpts from the diary of a communal apartment teen:

May 1, 1974

Today I lost the notebook of my poems and etudes. It hurts so much. Impossible to restore anything. Why do I value all these notes? Maybe I am just too self-involved and look for a "genius" inside me and am afraid to reconcile to the fact that I am just a very ordinary person and my life will also be very ordinary. But somewhere in my unconscious a thought bites at me (gryzet), that what if I become "talented," these notes might be needed for someone. They will be even a subject of discussion. Every person is most afraid to be ordinary and average (zauriadnym i riadovym) and secretly hopes that out of a million he might be the extraordinary one. This is ridiculous, absurd. Probably this requires from a person great will power, to stifle one's ambition, one's "I" and think about people around him, about the home. Are these high phrases? Can a person thinking just about himself be useful for the society and what kind of society would that be? Does it need this help?

I am waiting for something that would transform my life, but I don't have a big goal, except for an idle Manilov dream to be talented. One cannot live like that! You have to be sincere and honest even in trifles. I am sure I will never commit treason or back stabbing (podlost) on a large scale. But what about small villainy or a dirty trick (malenkaia podlost?) It's good that I can still evaluate my actions, without making them black or white.

Still, why is life so dirty? Why do they want to kill everything beautiful and pure? I won' t let it happen! I want to keep for the rest of my mind an impression of something beautiful, sublime, daring and not let anybody take it away from me. I want some miracle to come true.

I think it's over with S. I still hope for our meeting in Zelenogorsk, but there is not much hope. This year since we met was like a parody on true life. I don't have anything sacred left, I don't know what I believe in. I've lost interest in family holidays, New Year, spring vacations, birthdays. I have to "measure my desires to life" (Balzak, The Magic Skin). But my desires don't come to life like fairy tales. Maybe it's too early for them to come true? Maybe I was born too early or too late? That's why I live in the time of a lack of faith and contentment, the cult of things and possessions, and poverty, dimness (bednota, bleklost') of feelings. Maybe I exaggerate and life is still ahead of me? I want it to be interesting! I want to become somebody! Who? Who needs me?

Do I hope one day to become famous and for writing to be important? Who says so? Do I have too high an opinion of myself? And yet it is so important to do something useful in life, to become somebody ... I am just sitting here, life is so grey, so bleak ...

"It's dull to live in this world, ladies and gentleman" (Griboedov)

Why is life so dirty? I have to hold on to something beautiful, elevated, to keep me going ...

S. didn't call me. I know, I know I wrote this before. It's been a while since Zelenogorsk ... It was not real. Time to say good bye to the fairy tale ...

I live in the time of no-faith in anything (bezverie), contentment, the cult of things (kult veschej)

Or maybe I exaggerate? My whole life is ahead of me. I want it to be interesting! I want to become somebody, really, I want that very much. But who will I become? Who needs me?

June 12, 1974

The school year is over. All over. Emptiness. I waited for this day, waited impatiently … The exams are over, they were not so difficult. The last day. And suddenly it struck me. The year is over and nothing much happened to me? I am in the eighth grade! All hopes, all disappointments … Two smug mugs of the twins Trizniak's and Irka's very powdered face, that's all. We said goodbye for the summer like we see each other in an hour.

And now, "there is nothing I await from life. I experience something terrifying as if life repeats through centuries. The generation of poets who died during the Second World War, Vsevolod Bagristsky, Mayorov, were barely 25 and the Decembrist poets of the nineteenth century were 23–25. Our time is the time of Lermontov—emptiness and lack of spirit (bezduxovnost-)"

"With sadness I survey our present generation!

Their future seems so empty, dark, and cold,

Weighed down beneath a load of knowing hesitation,

in idleness stagnating, growing old …

And we both love and hate by chance, without conviction,

We make no sacrifice for malice, or for good.

There reigns within our souls a kind of chill constriction,

Whene'er the flame ignites the blood."

It seems that this is written about me.

Before bed, I feel like philosophizing, as usual. Just to distract, to think of this and that—just not about myself. About my "warm and complacent, well-fed" (syt) life, about loneliness and about S.

He doesn't think about me. Soon the moment will come when I go back to Zelenogorsk and will see him. And everything will be clear. Will he come up to talk to me? ...

If he doesn't come, I will get terribly upset.

He comes—I will forget him in a moment, but will have a feeling of well-fed (sytyj) satisfaction. Both versions are no good ... But as I am writing this, I think the second version is a bit better. I am a funny person, after all. Boredom.

"And life oppresses us, a flat road without meaning, An alien feast where we have dined." (Lermontov, Meditation)

And the best years of our lives are passing, all the best years. Dear Lermontov, You would have been able to understand me, but the centuries lie between us. You felt bad 150 years ago, and I feel bad now.

I wish there was school again, exams, worries. I am afraid to be alone with myself.

9th grade. September 9, 1974

I am almost an adult. I have to think about the future. And I "look at the future with fear and look at the past with longing" (Lermontov). I have to make decisions and figure out myself. Enough of the childish dreams of beautiful happiness that will be delivered to me on a little plate with a golden rim (na bliudechke s zolotoj kaemochkoj). I have to force through the road for myself, really force through (probivat). There are many people more talented than me. I am average, but I have to work on my capacities to the maximum. I have to work. My motto: more action. My future depends on me. To write, to work, to aspire (stremit-sia).

And all these romances (romany) distract me from that! They are not real, just funny and tragic. Why is everything repeating itself then? Why S. again? I know that he has someone real in his life and everything is impossible between us. I want to laugh at myself but I don't know how. I think I like him a little. And not the way it was last year (of course, there is still vanity there). I know I have to stop with S., to save my "nervous system." He likes me so little, only when I go with the flow and what would happen afterwards? Wouldn't it be funny to start 10th grade with the entry; 'S. again.'

****

My parents and grandparents were too scared to keep diaries. In Stalin's times a diary could be used to incriminate you for your thoughts and hints. Calls from barely identifiable S. and Yu. might be just as suspicious as the reflections on life's bleakness. Literary quotation mostly from the standard school program could have been seen as an Aesopian language. Who is this guy Lermontov to be so down on everything all the time? Soviet life in a 1970s communal apartment might not have struck a Western observer as characterized by "the cult of possessions" and contentment; there was more romantic struggle against the "domestic trash" in my family than there was "domestic trash" or treasure. To my surprise I find nothing about my parents in the diary and no description of our communal dwellings. There is no mention of the black entry to our house, the dark yard, the cheerful wallpaper of my room, the portiere and window curtains, the floor patterns, the art nouveau bas-relief on the high ceiling of my parents' room—all those material details that years later, in immigration I found so evocative.

There I was on the red pillows of my little bed made in Czechoslovakia, circa 1966, pouring my thoughts into yet another notebook, the color of military green. My chest of drawers is a total mess, not to be organized by any future archivist. Looking through the narrow unwashed window, or just staring into my eventless crumbling ceiling, I am waiting for the phone calls. S.? Yu.? If not now, when?

My perpetually drunk Aunt Shura is also waiting for my phone calls. When not working (which somehow was most of the time), she was lurking behind her door at the end of the corridor, ready to intercept all calls. Since S. rarely called and if he did, the conversation was short and practical, Aunt Shura didn't find him suspicious. (She didn't see his long foreign scarf clearly made in Finland.) It was my other "boyfriend" or rather phone-pal, Misha, that drew her interest and there I had to be vigilant. My relationship with Sasha was mostly about him not calling me and if he did call, it was about moving beyond talking (which I wasn't quite ready to do). Misha did call and we talked forever—to delay meeting.

Misha's deep hot voice is whispering into the communal receiver as I am sitting in the long corridor on an awkward chair playing the mental chess game on the black and white tiles of our floor. He tells me about Nietzsche and Napoleon and living above the bleak, corrupt everyday life. Aunt Shura walks around the corridor, back and forth, back and forth between her room and the kitchen. Carrying her teapot, then a cabbage pot and then carrying nothing just smiling maliciously. She would soon inform my parents about this dangerous phone call and a conversation about suspicious foreigners—maybe not even Jews, but worse: Nietzsche and Napoleon. And then I am back to my room watching drunks in my dark yard, or the familiar lonely exhibitionist who opens his raincoat to a scared female passerby. I see many people in hats looking down at their feet, at the puddles and trash in the asphalt yard, always looking down.

Black Entrance, 1986

In 1986 in Boston, I started to have dreams of my house. In one dream I stand in front of my house and I try to enter it but I can't. I don't remember what the doorknob looked like. In the dream I don't see the ornamental façade of my house on 79 Bolshoy Avenue. I rush quickly by the broken shards on the mosaic floor of the lobby and rush through the dark corridor fearing there is someone hiding behind the elevator right near the door of the mysterious office named Little Red Corner, the office of the Housing Committee, which seems to be forever locked or forever in the middle of a meeting. I am scared of a familiar ghost, a drunken man in the dark. I hear his resounding laughter followed by his stinking, spitting threats: "Fuck your mother in the mouth, you little bitch … Stinking ass." If I could only twist my tongue to repeat the curses, if I could only forgo my shameful intelligentsia habits and linger on every guttural sound "kh" the drunkard would stop laughing at me. I could enter my house fearlessly and give the hallway stranger a wink of complicity. I could have been home by now. My compressed lips are ready for the forceful "u" sound, my throat is about to utter the guttural sound. But somehow, the air is blocked, the sound freezes on my lips and my obscenities remain mute, harmless, unheard and unheard-of defenseless.

There were two ways to enter our communal apartment: from the backwater of Karpovka River, on Petropavlovsky Street, 4, you enter into the yard and then proceed to our dark staircase in its corner. The other way was more glamorous. On Bolshoy Prospekt 79 you see a grey neo-baroque façade with bay windows and statues not far from the famous art nouveau buildings with a fantastic gothic tower. You enter into a lobby with bas-reliefs and mosaics, the cosmopolitan style of the turn of the twentieth century that one encounters all over the world. There was, of course, no doorman there in the Soviet era and you would proceed at your own risk on the ruined mosaics and shards of broken glass into another unlit passage that led to the courtyard.

The entrance that I had just failed to take used to be the main entrance to the house. It was a typical fantastic building of the turn-of-the-century cosmopolitan architecture that combined neo-baroque façades, Roman masks, magic birds and historical ornaments from different époques. In our case, we had to go through that building in order to get to the interior yard from where you take a back entrance up to our place. To enter the communal apartment requires a long rite of passage: in and out through a dark hallway with ruined mosaics and broken beer bottles and across the interior yards full of communal trash, with occasional graffiti and half-erased hopscotch on the asphalt. Visiting a Soviet home, one is struck not only by a deep contrast between the public and private spheres, and by that strange no-man's land, the space that belongs to everybody and to nobody, but creates discomfort in both public and private existence. The hallway occupies a special place in the Soviet mythical topography; it is a space of transition, a space of fear, the dark limit of the house. It could preserve traces of a building's former elegance: fragments of mosaics and ruined, not-so-classical pilasters with obscene graffiti scribbled all over. The hallways are usually inhabited by old drunks, local fools, youth gangs and teenagers in love. Here all sorts of unofficial initiations take place. At best there would be a few romantic kisses with poems of Lermontov or Esenin and a benevolent rant of the local war veterans with a bottle of Stolichnaya. For the darker side, we would have to picture all sorts of unreported crimes happening in the hallways from rape to murder, committed in a state of total intoxication.

The Soviet bard Bulat Okudzhava dedicated a song to communal "black staircases" inhabited by black cats and ghosts of fear. The black entrance to the communal apartments leads to a dark corner of the Soviet unconscious. In the song the black cat that "never cries nor sings" embodies the suspicions of Stalin's times, the mutual fears and occasional tragic complicity of informants and victims who often inhabited the same communal apartment. The end of the song is a poetic reflection on the Soviet collective mentality. All it will take is "to put a new light bulb on the black staircase"—one collective illumination, metaphorically speaking, and then some of the dark fears can be eliminated. But somehow collective inaction conspires to keep the public spaces dark. The black staircase is an unofficial Soviet public site, not iconographic like the Metro or palaces of culture; this in-between was everybody's and therefore nobody's responsibility. It was on the outskirts of the visible Soviet topography.

My house, a typical old St. Petersburgian building partitioned into many communal apartments, was located on Bolshoy Avenue near the Karpovka River, which in the nineteenth century constituted the urban frontier. The building was rumored to have belonged to a wealthy St. Petersburg engineer, a nouveau riche with a non-Russian name and cosmopolitan, eclectic tastes. For me the cosmopolitan façade of my building was my private "window into Europe." Somehow it made me feel that by osmosis I belonged to a larger "nostalgia for world culture" reflected in the façades of my city. I could walk all the way on Bolshoy Avenue or on Kirovsky Avenue decorated by these incredible buildings that mimicked all styles—from Greco-Roman, to baroque, from neo classical, to Moorish and from there to the late Stalinist Art Deco. This was a living history book for me to inhabit. Joseph Brodsky wrote that he learned more about world culture from the Petersburg façades than from books. The city was not fully censored; it belonged to all of us and no propaganda posters could disfigure it.

After the Revolution all the apartments on Bolshoy 79 were subdivided with partitions and "densified" by the additional neighbors. As for the original owner, he was forever erased from history and from the well-kept list of house residents in the Building Committee Office. (It was rumored that he was a Cadet. He even collaborated with the revolutionary government. But around 1926 he obtained a foreign passport and "went traveling." He may have died of consumption on the French Riviera with a little volume of Pushkin's poems in his hands. Perhaps he suffered a heart attack in a small Mexican village while making love to a beautiful member of the local Trotskyist group ... I am glad he did not turn into an anonymous neighbor in the partitioned and subdivided apartment on the third floor, vanishing in the purges of 1937 or 1942.) With the engineer's disappearance, the single narrative of the house bifurcates into the fragmented tales of the countless neighbors in the communal apartments. I am as forgotten in the books of the now defunct Housing Committee as is everyone else. Only the whimsical eclectic façade remains whole, defiantly incompatible with the new Soviet style.

In the late 1970s I worked as a Leningrad tour guide, mostly for the Young Pioneers from provincial towns. "Leningrad, Petersburg, Petrograd—these three names tell the whole history of our Soviet city-hero." The first line of our memorized tour had an obligatory notation: the voice rises on every name of the city and falls on the "hero." The tourist agency "Sputnik" was located not far from Bolshoy Avenue and the bus often passed near my house. The goal of the tour was to take the visitors away from the Petersburg cosmopolitan eclecticism to the classical ensembles on the squares around Neva, the monuments to Lenin with his hand outstretched and the revolutionary cruiser Aurora. But the tourists couldn't help themselves and would get excited by the exotic birds and masks on my street. "This building on Bolshoy," I was supposed to say (condemning ascending note) "with strange beasts on the façade derives from foreign models, lacks classical proportions, and does not present any real architectural value." Occasionally, I would add a wink of complicity there that would make the value of Leningrad masks skyrocket in a flash.

October 13, 1975

God, how sad. I feel the no-exit situation and aimlessness of existence (bezvyxodnost- I bezysxodnost sususchestvovania). Also, all my hurts and small "unhappiness"—are all trifles in the face of real human suffering. Maybe it's just the whining that comes with my age? I have to suffer through it, how can it be otherwise; I just need S. or Yu. to call me and just talk in a human way. It's just a small thing I need for my equilibrium and then I can write and believe again. About my so-called writing (naschet moej pisaniny)—too many ideas and too little will power, discipline and time. They say that life is like a chess board and you walk on white or black squares. I've been walking on black ones for too long. And sometimes I think it's a grey square equally distant from black and white.

Now I believe in my ambition. Here is an interesting idea.

"I want to live for immortality and don't accept a partial compromise." Dostoevsky, Brothers Karamazoff

And what if in my life I would have to accept the partial compromise? Sad.

October 14, Sunday

A little bit of statistics, as Mayakovsky wrote, there are many professions, good and different (xoroshix I raznyx). This October here are my plans about institutes.

1. Institute of Nadezhda Krupskaya, technical translation.

2. Herzen Pedagogical, Mathematics in English

3. Theater Institute, directing Leningrad University, Czech or Polish philology.

Really, I dream all the time about Leningrad University, journalism philology, psychology, but I know it's off limits to me, it's a "forbidden fruit."

Everything is normal. Neither gay, nor sad, there is a routine, waiting for evenings, vacations, study, entertain myself. As usual. A little bit edgy when the phone rings, but in general Vse, all right (all right in English) ... Long live the everydayness!

January 15, 1975

Happy New Year! This year should be merry! At midnight I laughed after having drunk just half a glass of champagne. It should be a calm year, for a person needs so little to be merry. And now I will advertise my new theory.

Evolution, its driving forces or "Svetlana Goldberg, and her role in the Russian Revolution."

We, the people invented thousands of conventions, wars, borders and kinds of national territories and social systems. But only one thing is eternal, the humaneness in human beings. What I mean is not reason, but what is conventionally called "heart." But heart as an anatomic organ has nothing to do with it. "Heart" is the realm of humaneness. This is our only treasure, love, friendship, loyalty to our convictions. Everyone loved—the heroes of Homer, Shakespeare, Puskin, we love and so will our descendants. People loved during the feudal social regime, during slavery, capitalism and socialist regimes. People loved, were possessed by doubt, sought after truth, higher truth (pravda, istina.) But people loved differently, the culture of love and human relationships is changing. And that's the process of evolution. All technical achievements are but means for the goal (vozvyshenie) of a human being and world harmony. It's a utopia, a fairy tale, but there is an element of truth here. If we preserve a primordial human nature, happiness is possible. And all the vanity and egoism are testimony to the rotting of the society. Society (of any kind) develops "by fits and starts" (in English). Just progress is impossible.

End to part 1 (like in a good detective story).

Continue. This is called I am looking for justice. Came to the conclusion: there is no absolute justice. What people call Justice might seem like living without compromises, but it can also be to their advantage. Too much "uncompromising" or too much profit—neither would work.

My motto:

"Subject everything to doubt!" Karl Marx.

I am concerned about social problems, I want to take part in governing, the state, to contribute to the society (of honest people), not to feel myself "second class." I don't want to compromise! I want to be honest, even when this goes beyond the conventional frame (ramki obshepriniatogo). Honest to the bottom, but it's not always possible and not always nice to the people around me.

A Homecoming, 1991–2015

Ten years after I left the USSR, I finally entered the dark courtyard of my house—and that was no dream. The main entrance was blocked, and on the broken glass door an outdated poster advertised a video salon featuring Rambo II, Emmanuelle and a Brazilian soap opera, The Slave Isaura Part IV. The first impression was disappointing. The house looked like a mere lookalike. "What is happening here?" I asked an elderly woman standing on the street where there used to be a bus stop. "Repairs," she answered.

So, I failed to enter my house through Bolshoy 79 and had to sneak in through the broken wooden fence on the other side of the yard. I was surrounded by heaps of trash, telephone wires, pieces of old furniture, worn-out slippers, the pages of a 1979 calendar, mysterious schedules and graphics, all fragments of the perfect technical organization of labor whose purpose was now entirely lost, along with pieces of a broken record by a once-popular French singer of the 1960s. Yes, it's him, Adamo. "Tombait la neige / Tu ne viendrais pas ce soir / Tombait la neige / Tout est blanc de désespoir."

Climbing through the trash, I made my way upstairs. Some of the partitions had been taken down, and the whole framework of our interpersonal and communal interactions was broken. All the wrong doors, which once were locked and hidden behind the wallpaper to keep separate entrances for the neighbors, were open. The communal kitchen, our apartment forum, seemed to have shrunk in size, and so had our interminable corridor, where the communal telephone once hung. The apartment looked like an abandoned stage set.

Suddenly I looked up in disbelief. That floral bas-relief on the ceiling in my parents' room was still there, with the exposed wire where the lamp once was. In a painted window frame on the yellow wallpaper, a vase of flowers and an open book on the sill, and an empty center in the middle, there used to be a glossy poster of a view from a window of a faraway Mediterranean country, something like Crimea, only abroad. The window frame immediately brought back memories. It was painted by my then husband, Kostya, during the brief six months in the 1980s when we lived with my parents. We were in limbo then, not sure whether to become refugees or refuseniks. The apartment had been already slated for repairs and the neighbors got another place to live while we continued in the familiar disrepair. The dark room did not have a window and we used to joke that this poster was our "window to Europe." It was our last fantastic plan; should we be refused the visa; we could become escape artists and move through the painted frame to the mythical West. The poster itself was gone but the frame still evoked our liminal selves.

I approached the kitchen window into the yard: black balconies with holes were still precariously attached to the building and a few uprooted plants continued to inhabit them. An old lonely drunk wandered into the gaping hole of the back entrance. He stopped to urinate near the skeleton of the old staircase. And then I look out: in the center of the yard there was an old truck, as if from World War II and there was one huge graffiti on the wall: DEATH. I frame it just the way it is.

****

Next day after visiting my house, I went to see my best high-school girlfriend Kycha, with whom I shared so many adventures in our early teenage years.

"Remember that little park where we buried our secrets? It has been privatized now. You can't go to that part."

"I have something for you," she added suddenly and gave me a pile of green notebooks with Pushkin's silhouette and multiplication tables in the back.

"Your diaries."

I reread them for first time in twenty years, on a bleak March day in 2015. To my surprise I relate to my earlier writing much more than to the building in which I lived, even though it is our communal apartment that appeared to me in my dream and which I explored obsessively in my work. Maybe now I can extend my hand now to that little Soviet dreamer, all embarrassment apart. I am still scribbling in my corner, dispersing myself in virtual bites, making sense of the small data. Ok, my home is bigger, but X. still didn't call. And humanity remains endangered. (Emoticon, smile. My teenage self would so disapprove!)

I couldn't bring the diary into immigration. But I carried with me what was mine: the emerging voice, the turn of a phrase, the interior designs. I changed languages but not always the ways of storytelling. Our secret self is like an immigrant trickster who plays hide-and-seek with us and yet persists through continuities and gaps with an accented integrity.

At the end, the diary was a better holder of memories and forgetting than the architecture of the former home. "Forever you, the unwashed Russia! The land of slaves the land of lords: And you, the blue-uniformed ushers, And people who worship them as gods." Lermontov, who else.

****

I returned to America and showed my parents my photograph of our yard with the word "Death" scribbled on the wall. They seemed remarkably unfazed. It was back in 1990 and they had left the Soviet Union only three years earlier and felt no nostalgia. "We heard from friends that they were making a movie in our yard. Lenfilm studios, I think. And they brought an old truck in and left it there. It must have been something about the war and the Leningrad blockade."

"No, no, it was a film about the poet Daniil Kharms who lived somewhere nearby. He wrote about a man who left his house with a cane and a sack and … never came back." One day in 1937 Daniil Kharms left his house to buy a pack of cigarettes and never came back …

4

Tearing Away

Foreword and translation by Natal'ya Strugach

Foreword

Some people have a special gift for inspiring others to create. Meeting someone from this stratum is a stroke of luck, and becoming their friend is a real fortune. Svetlana Boym—Harvard professor, scholar of cultural studies and Slavic literature, writer, photographer and artist—belonged to this rare class of inspiring people. Our friendship began when we were still children. Talking to her always made me feel recharged by a life-giving energy which made it easier to think and to breathe.

We were in the same grade at Leningrad school #80. Svetlana began to use her writing to make sense of the world when she was ten or eleven. She wrote in her journal—swashbuckler stories, epigrams, poems. Sometimes we would write together, especially in the spring, sitting on a bench in a park on Kirovsky Prospekt.[1] I still have some of the funny poems and sketches we worked on.

The title of the story was chosen by Natal'ya Strugach, a classmate and friend of Svetlana who here writes the foreword.

[1] One of the main streets of the Petrogradsky District of Saint Petersburg, it is now named Kammenoostrovsky Prospekt.

Svetlana studied Spanish philology at the Herzen State Pedagogical University. In the summer of 1979, she met the young Moscow architect Konstantin Boym in Koktebel'. They got married that winter. Kostya was planning to emigrate to America, and Svetlana decided to go with him. She dropped out of her program (she was in her fourth year at the time), threw away her Komsomol membership card, worked odd jobs as a translator and tour guide and went back and forth between Moscow and Leningrad. It took almost a year before the couple received official permission to leave the country, and she spent that entire time in constant worry and anticipation. The story we have here is about that period of her life. In 1981 Svetlana and Konstantin were allowed to leave the USSR, and after several months in Italy, they finally made it to America. There, Sveta accomplished a great deal: she got a scholarship to study at Boston University, she wrote and defended her dissertation, became a tenured professor at Harvard, wrote several highly regarded books of scholarship, as well as a play, a novel and many stories. Her books have been translated into many different languages. You can read all about this on Wikipedia. To me, she remained the dearest of friends.

When Sveta left for America, she gave me her handwritten journal because she wasn't allowed to leave the country with it. In the 1990s, when she came to Russia as a tourist, I returned it to her. Unfortunately, the journal was lost after her death in 2015. I still have a copy of the story published here, which she wrote right before she emigrated. It's unfinished, and it was written by a 21-year-old girl, not a Harvard professor. I am certain that she never planned on publishing it later, when she was already a professional writer. But after thinking about it, and talking to Sveta's parents, I decided to publish it. Now that Svetlana is no longer with us, her writing is all the more interesting and valuable, and this story captures so well the oppressive atmosphere of Soviet Moscow, the heaviness of fear and unfreedom. Moreover, from a psychological point of view, this story is an interesting example of the interior life of a young woman who is planning to leave for good—because when people left back then, they left for good. The protagonist repudiates everything that surrounds her, and her sadness is akin to a deep depression: she feels unwanted and rejected by the people, the city, the country, and she senses malevolent, judgmental eyes on her wherever she goes. She is no longer really *here*, but not yet *there* either. Her family is her only source of strength and support. How can it be that the rare ability to inspire others can coexist with such feelings of discomfort, sadness, solitude? Talented people often have to contend with this paradox.

Svetlana Boym died in 2015, aged fifty-six. She was very sick, she knew that she was probably going to die, but she kept writing articles and stories until almost the very end. Starting in the 1990s, Svetlana only wrote in English. Right now, there's a large effort to translate her books into Russian. My son, Aleksandr Strugach, translated one of her most important scholarly books, *The Future of Nostalgia*, which will soon be published. Her final stories, written in English, were about our childhood, about Russia. I have begun to translate them into Russian; maybe they too will be published. And now we are publishing Sveta's first story, written in Russian.

The story is untitled. I would title it "Tearing Away."

[I present it to you here and I hope you will read it generously and with understanding. The spelling and punctuation of the author have been preserved.]

****

The wolfhound age springs at my shoulders
though I'm no wolf by blood.

—OSIP MANDELSHTAM[2]

I

Moscow, rush hour at the tram stop. A dark autumn wind, the weather is damp and oppressive. A tram comes slowly around the turn. The crowd becomes

---

[2]Translation by Clarence Brown and W. S. Merwin.

agitated, a giant mass of grey or dark brown coats, jackets, bags, it starts to move, rushing toward the narrow half-open door.

A large woman with a mohair beret and a short woolen coat, looking like a school head mistress, shoves her way past a red-eyed young man whose tie is sticking out: "Why do young people always get on before everyone else?"

A tipsy guy in his fifties steps on the foot of a young woman in a black leather coat, "O hello, miss," and sweeps her aside.

Two stocky middle-aged men with briefcases – "It's always so crowded" – push him and rush toward the front. Somebody steps aside to make room for an old lady, hunched and grimacing, a stuffed string bag in her hands. She is clambering up up up with all her might.

People are pushing through in ever greater numbers. Now groups of three, five, six at a time are getting in. It's no longer a matter of individual willpower, there's a special force at play, the will of the crowd, an aggregate of accelerations, shoves, elbows. And some slight adjustments: "Hey you, move into the car," "don't crush me," "put away your umbrella." After some effort, the final sentence has been passed: the door of the tram closes with a screech. The last person on is a girl with a knit hat slipping off her head, her dark hair showing underneath.

This is me. I got into the tram. I make my way deeper into the car, hide in the corner by the ticket machine. I am now part of the collective, and I immediately enter into a special system of relations with all of its happy members.

I am standing by the ticket machine, which, of course, means I have to do the honors: to put in money and tear off tickets. It's a special kind of ritual: "Could you be so kind," "please, pass it on," "if you could please, two tickets" (the politeness is staggering! A minute ago, we were all elbowing each other). "I only have ten kopecks … two tickets … Thank you, I don't need any change."

I smile. I am also polite. But I'm the only one who does not pay. Who would I pay? And for what? Of course, I clench 3 kopecks in my pocket just in case, so that I'm ready if the need arises. The people standing next to me seem to read my thoughts: they look at me with unfriendly suspicion. This frightens me, I step away from the ticket machine and make my way to the cold iron armrest of a seat.

The members of the tram collective have certain rights and responsibilities, as well as their freedoms. Here, as in Hyde Park, you can talk about lots of things. The crush creates a sense of intimacy: any conversation can be heard, can be joined, and is in no way binding.

At first, they talk about some things we don't have. Two women with packed bags:

"Hullo. So, did you manage?"

"You know, I stood there for another two hours after I saw you, they ran out right when I got to the front."

"Tough luck. You should go to the *universam*[3] around eight in the morning."

"Yesterday I waited in line for cheese. And there wasn't any! And before that ham, salted pork."

"Don't even start! My sister came from Tula. Each person gets 200 grams of butter!"

"We're feeding the entire world. And we had to host the Olympics!"

"But we did a great job at the Olympics. I saw the closing ceremony. Beautiful! It was so well organized!"

"We watched it in color at my neighbors'. Our guys shut everyone up!"

On the other side, a large man in a fox hat and a woman in her forties with very regular features talk about the things we do have:

She: "People live so well nowadays: everyone has an apartment, a rug, a color television. No one goes hungry."

He, with skepticism: "People just have a lot of money. No one lives off their salary. Take salespeople, waiters, and others too …"

"Come on, there are very few people like that."

---

[3]Supermarket; this acronym (from "universal self-service store," "universal'nyi magazin samoobsluzhivaniia") has been used since 1970.

A fat little man bravely enters the conversation:

"Everyone's lying, alright? What, like you don't know? They're lying!"

The drunk man, like the medieval jester, can always speak his mind. He will be forgiven; he is entirely harmless.

I stay quiet, I smile, look around. Conversations on the tram always break unexpectedly and at the most interesting moments. People love variety here. A minute later everyone's attention and enthusiasm turns toward a girl who failed to give up her seat for someone. Yelps of outrage, hissing, judgment. I make my way toward the exit, people are shoving me from all sides, as if saying goodbye, their elbows catch my side, my back, my stomach.

The tram stops. People fly out like peas spilling from a jar. A minute ago, we were its contents, and that brought us together. A minute later and we slither off alone down the dark, damp streets. I continue the conversation in my head.

"Yes, there is no meat. Yes, they're lying. Yes, there are carpets, but …"

But I cannot allow myself the sincerity of the tram, my situation is different.

I walk faster. I am scared to walk by myself down this dark street. Both sides are lined with the giant white rectangles of apartment buildings. I walk past them like they're a line of soldiers. I can feel the piercing gaze of their symmetrical windows. There is light in them. Hundreds of tiny cookie-cutter apartment-cells, in which all kinds of different people watch the same movie on their TVs (some in color, some black and white). And on the blue screen brave *chekists*[4] overcome each and every hurdle, and expose a dangerous conspiracy by parasites and enemies of the state.

I live in an older building. I walk through the narrow well of the inner courtyard, and climb up to our apartment on the fourth floor. I am greeted by the deafening blare of the radio.

"All that nonsense propaganda about how détente is threatened by the Soviet Union violating the Helsinki Accords …" I turn down the volume. It's

---

[4] A *chekist* is an official working for the *Cheka*, the name of the Soviet state security organization from 1918–22, or any of its later descendants.

alright, my grandmother had turned it up, they'll do the weather report after the news, and she doesn't even know how cold it is today.

Everyone's already home. Mom is on the phone in the hallway.

"Yes, definitely stop by. Allochka just got home."

"At the institute? It's fine. She's taking her exams."

"Yes, she'll be done next year."

"Thanks, I'll tell her."

That, of course, is about me. Except that I am no longer at the institute and I am not taking any exams. I had to withdraw from the program when my husband and I submitted the documents to leave the country, but my mom doesn't like to talk about this, and she always makes up stories about my exams and papers.

You can hear every phone conversation at home. Walking through the hallway, people feel obliged to add their two cents. Dad turns on the record player. Dixon, "Texts and Dialogues," spills out from under the door and asks in Russian-English: "*When you finish your talk?*"

I am sad, I don't feel like doing anything, I yell back from my room: "*When do you finish your talk?*"

I go to my dad.

"*Yes?*" He asks.

"Daddy, *do you finish*, it's a question!"

"Alright, *do you finish*, what's the difference? You're not practicing with us at all."

"I will, I will," I tell him. (My husband is out of town for two days, and I promised to spend them with my parents.) I pick up the textbook – Bonk, volume one. Dad is reading a touching story about the encounter between Mr. Smith and comrade Petrov. "*Mr. Smith is a great friend of the Soviet Union, comrade Petrov would like to show him Lenin's Mausoleum on the Red Square.*" Mister Smith "*is very happy*," he loves Moscow and its giant squares and new neighborhoods. He's especially taken with Gorky street, which "*after the Great October Socialist Revolution*" transformed from a narrow street into a central artery.

I start asking him questions about the text:

"Who is mister Smith?"
"He is an Englishmen. He is a friend of our country."
"Who is comrade Petrov?"
"He is a KGB agent!"

We burst out laughing. Our laughter summons my mom. She also speaks English and doesn't want to miss anything. "*Meine Tochter speak English only with father.*" (My mom studied German in school and loves to show off her knowledge of both languages.) My parents used to find English a nightmare – what's the point of breaking your tongue, contorting it between your teeth, making ridiculous sounds, why not just speak plainly, like in Russian?

Now they're used to it, they've stopped asking stupid questions. To them English is a game with its own rules and restrictions, a sad game, because they are forced to fold complex thoughts into simple short sentences, but still a fun game, like a child's set of building blocks.

As usual, the "lesson" doesn't last long. Dad wants to surprise us and, as if by chance, turns on the tape player. We hear the hissing, rustling crackle of a worn-out tape. And suddenly, out of the past, out of the shapeless scraps of sound, emerge the guitar chords and the piercing, awfully familiar intonation of Okudzhava:

Ah, what marvelous nights,
But my mom is sad and worried.
Son, why do you walk
so alone,
so alone?

I hold the roads of April end to end.
The stars have grown so large and kind ...
Mom, I am on duty,
I must attend
to April[5]

This song is twenty years old but it still strikes the same secret sadness about something mysterious, and now entirely impossible.

The room is swimming in front of my eyes, the decorations are changing. I see the old garish wallpaper, the heavy curtains and the tiny television set in the corner. Behind the wall, our half-drunk neighbor is snoring again. We're all living in the same room: me, my mom and my dad. In the corner, behind a curtain, are my little bed and table, color pencils and open books strewn all around. My parents have guests over. They are dancing, laughing, listening to Okudzhava, or maybe Vysotsky:

Why would she think of me, she's already in Paris,
Marcel Marceau himself is talking to her now ...[6]

My parents are young, happy.

The sixties ... The upheaval is behind us, and soon everything should be alright. There are exhibits of impressionist art, books about modern painting. Mom and dad bought a giant Degas nude and hung it over the bed. Grandma gasped in horror when she first saw it (though Degas is her contemporary). And when they asked little Alla, "who's your favorite artist?" she answered, without a moment's thought, "Ivan Gogh!"

Everyone goes to hear Voznesensky, Akhmadulina, Evtushenko[7], everyone is reading Aksyonov and Hemingway. My parents sold all of their old furniture

---

[5]Bulat Okudzhava, "Dezhurny po apreliu" ("A Patrolman of April").
[6]Vladimir Vysotsky, "Ona byla v Parizhe" ("She'd Been to Paris").
[7]These poets' readings drew huge crowds in the 1960s, during the Khrushchev Thaw.

except for three stools. They hung something resembling a fisherman's net on the window, "so that there's more light."

The radio promises communism in twenty years. But something is starting to crack, to break. I remember a vacation in Crimea, my parents gathered with their friends every night, they would listen to the Voice of America and have lively discussions. Unrest in Czechoslovakia. How will this end, what kind of changes were coming?

I was shaped by the 70s. We'd heard stories about the Stalin years, and the echoes of the sixties still reached us. In high school, we listened, mesmerized, to the Beatles and Jesus Christ Superstar, and dreamed of wearing faded jeans.

Five years later we could buy a new pair of name-brand blue jeans for a hefty sum, roughly the equivalent of one month's salary for a Soviet engineer. Our attitude toward contemporary music became more critical. Disco and Boney M evoked a mocking smile. I overlapped with the last of the hippies, but they seemed completely disillusioned and tattered. They would turn before your very eyes into black market hucksters or else the usual engineers and heads of families. We were skeptics even in high school, snickering at the ornate phrases in history and literature textbooks, but still able to repeat them when necessary, articulating each word with great pathos. We were formalists, we didn't have the tiniest bit of enthusiasm, and older generations saw this clearly.

Everything flows, everything changes. In our old room (now just my parents' room), there is new wallpaper, and the heavy curtain is gone. The Degas nude has been replaced by some kind of landscape in a gilded frame. French vases, a gift from my grandmother for my parents' wedding, sit atop the piano. They had spent twenty-five years in a heap on a shelf, and now my mother is dusting them every day and talking about them – are they from the 18th or 19th century? It's good that my parents haven't lost their sense of time. Five years ago, my dad did not say goodbye to his friend, who was leaving for Israel, and now he completely understands the choice I've made. But their sympathies still lie with the past, and Okudzhava and Vysotsky are still playing today, except Vysotsky is newer, from a French record:

Heat up the banya, in black –
I've grown so unused to this world –
I will burn, I'll go mad in the heat,
and the steam will loosen my tongue[8]

Two months ago, Vysotsky died of a heart attack. Aksyonov left for America, and Okudzhava is writing elegant historical novels:

in a dark glass
under imported beer
a red rose blossomed
slowly and proudly
we write as we hear
we hear as we breathe
we breathe so we write
not trying to please ...[9]

My parents are scared now. My mom was already called to the first department.[10] When someone is studying English and complaining of heart trouble, that's not a good sign. Some of her coworkers have stopped saying hello to her just in case, others have been looking at her with hostility (or maybe she is imagining it?). Her old friend knows all of this and feels bad for her, but makes sure to call us from a payphone, "so that nothing comes of it."[11] Their circle of friends grows more and more narrow.

---

[8] Vladimir Vysotsky, "Ban'ka po Belomu" ("Heat the Banya"). The original lyrics are "heat up the banya in white."
[9] Bulat Okudzhava, "I'm writing a historical novel." This song was dedicated to the novelist Vasily Aksyonov.
[10] The First Department ("pervyi otdel") was in charge of the political security of Soviet workplaces.
[11] This popular expression describing excessive caution ("kak by chego ne vyshlo"/"what if something happened") comes from Anton Chekhov's story *The Man in a Case* ("Chelovek v futliare"), in which the protagonist is exceedingly cautious and judgmental of those who behave improperly.

Ring ring ring. The phone interrupts my thoughts, rings for a long time, boring and demanding. Finally, mom picks it up. I've recently lost my taste for talking on the phone. It's always the same. All of my phone conversations fall into one of two categories.

First category:

"Hello."

"Hello."

"How are things?"

"You know …"

"Still in school?"

"Still in school."

"Taking your exams?"

"Taking my exams."

"It's going okay?"

"It's going okay."

Second category:

"Hello."

"Hello."

"How are things?"

"You know …"

"Still waiting?"

"Still waiting."

"How long has it been?"

"Seventeen months (eighteen, nineteen, twenty …)."

"You went to the OVIR?[12]"

---

[12] The OVIR ("Otdel viz i registratsii," "Office of Visas and Registration") was the Soviet Ministry of Internal Affairs department responsible for issuing exit visas to Soviet citizens seeking to emigrate. Starting in the late 1960s, many Soviet Jewish citizens applied for exit visas to emigrate to Israel (and, later, the United States). Many cases would languish in the OVIR for years; the popular term for those denied an exit visa was "refusenik" ("otkaznik").

"Nothing?"

"Nothing."

This time it's my friend Nina calling. She loves mysteries of all kinds.

"Hello."

"Hello."

"Oh, I have some news."

"Okay?"

"My parents and I went to the hospital today. They won't let us see my cousin."

"What? Who's in the hospital?" (This is a new development, and I'm feeling lost.)

"You don't get it?"

"I don't get it."

"Alright, I'll call again later."

I spend some time mulling over the mysterious code of Nina's words. Soon enough they line up in a simple and logical manner. Nina is scared to talk directly – which means this is about documents. The hospital is OVIR; the rest is all clear, they got an invitation from their cousin, but their documents are not being accepted. A new ruse, a new trap, another turn in the endless maze, which is near impossible to get through. I know that soon enough Nina and I, and someone else will meet up, will talk at length about what we can do, and probably come to the conclusion that we should just do something, we should go to various offices, write letters, do whatever we can. We will even write one of the thousands of letters that goes nowhere, and as usual, they won't dignify us with an answer.

And time keeps passing, and we wait longer and longer. We are still caught in a complicated spiderweb of relationships and compromises, hypocrisy and fear. Except our cards are all on the table. The giant secretive machine could start moving at any moment and decide our fate. Some man with a closely-cropped haircut and a soldier's bearing will walk into the right office and pick our file off the right shelf. He will open it and make a decision with a stroke of the pen. And what exactly governs him? His personal striving or the will of the giant machine, where thousands of compromises intersect, thousands of plans and circumstances! We try to guess what they might be. Who will be the next president of the US? What will they decide in Madrid? Are they trying to silence the Voice of America broadcast? What's happening in Poland? Who will go from faraway Tehran to faraway Baghdad? So many different circumstances have to fall into just the right pattern, which will then set the machine into motion. We will never know which drop made the glass overflow.

The radio is still on in the kitchen. "The Washington hawks have long tried to rope their allies into a despicable venture: to disturb the present power equilibrium in the hopes of gaining military advantage over the Soviet Union. As for the USSR, like Leonid Ilych Brezhnev said in November, he is in favor of preserving détente, of extending it, of a peaceful and equal collaboration between governments …"

Yet another evening discussion by yet another political commentator. This too is a part of our lives, our constant accompaniment. It's the background to our dinners, our conversations, our thoughts. Grandma interacts with the radio more than the rest of us. She is at war with it, she curses it, she argues with it. Sometimes she will spend hours by the radio just listening to some Beethoven symphony or Tchaikovsky concert. But if you step into the kitchen right at twelve, when my parents are already sleeping, you will see the following picture: grandma, bent over the kitchen table, pulling at the radio antenna, turning all the knobs at once, muttering to herself, as if casting a spell. She's trying to catch her favorite "Broadcast for midnighters." The radio emits only noise, crackle, and some barely discernible phrases in a distinctly non-Russian intonation. But grandma is still happy, now she can really, truly talk to her heart's content. Grandma curses everything, starting with world politics and ending with contemporary fashion and music. I often make fun of her for it, though I probably shouldn't.

My grandma is a member of the longest-suffering generation, the one born at the turn at the century. Her older brothers used to go to meetings of the Free Philosophical Association and attend Chaliapin premiers.[13] Her first childhood love was shot at age 18 for being a Kadet.[14] That was in 1919. Grandma never finished university, but spent her entire life working in schools. In 1937, her husband was sent to prison, and they never saw each other again. Then came war, evacuation, hunger.

In 1948 grandma was arrested. My dad and his sister raised themselves. And in 1953, a couple of days after Stalin died, grandma received the following letter in prison from her son: "Mommy, oh god, what a loss! I almost didn't go to the funeral, but …"

Soon after, grandma was released and rehabilitated, and life slowly went back to normal. But an oppressive fear and distrust still lingers in her heart. It is still there many years later, grandma doesn't believe in the possibility of leaving, she's scared to even talk about it. Why, she still remembers how in 1914 her older brother was planning to leave for America.

Many Jews left at the time. It was a normal everyday occurrence – back then. But now is a very different time. It's hard for me to talk to her about this. She is scared for me.

I sit in the kitchen with grandma, together we cast spells over the radio receiver, I press the buttons, I pull the antenna. All we get in response is crackling noise and snippets of upbeat music. Today the "Broadcast for midnighters" has been cancelled due to technical difficulties. We tell each other good night and go to bed.

---

[13] The Free Philosophical Association ("Vol'naia filosofskaia assotsiatsiia" or "Vol'fila") was a cultural organization based in Petersburg (with branches in Moscow and Berlin) active from 1919–24, which held lectures and discussions on topics of art and culture through the lens of philosophy and the tenets of socialism. Many prominent members of the intelligentsia frequented these meetings; the Association was led by the writers Ivanov-Razumnik and Bely. Feodor Chaliapin was a famous Russian opera singer.

[14] The Constitutional Democratic Party ("Konstitutsionno-demokraticheskaia partiia" or "K-D," thus the name "Kadets"/"Cadets" for its members) was a liberal political party in the Russian Empire. After the October Revolution, the party was suppressed by the Bolshevik government.

II

The next morning. I sit in bed and look out the window. I can see a small scrap of grey sky and the curved black lines of empty balconies. The bright colors of laundry hanging in some of them, half-frozen plants lining others.

I like this inner courtyard: in spite of everything, it has its own special character and stands out amidst all the other identical small courtyard-wells.

As always, Sunday morning begins with the ring of the telephone. I run out to the corridor, but mom got there first. I can tell by her tense expression that the conversation is about me:

"Yes, she's taking her exams."

"All's well, thank you."

"Yes, her husband is travelling for work."

Yes, all is well.

All is good, all is normal, all is fine. My poor mother! A minute later, the phone rings again. This time I get it.

"Hello. How's it going?"

"Fine."

"You coming?"

"I'm coming. Four o'clock?"

"Yes."

I completely forgot, today we have that most noteworthy event – a class reunion. It's not hard to guess what will happen, we meet up every year. The first moments – oohs and aahs and joy. We will drink. Misha Voskresenskii, the life of the party who once would recite Esenin's "The Black Man," will bring the coolest records, share witty anecdotes about his district party committee job, and promise to bring us all Ceylon tea and Finnish cervelat.

Tanya Gellerman, "the brightest girl in school," will talk about a popular novel published in the latest issue of *Foreign literature*. She never managed to get into the literature department at the university, finally her parents shoved her into the Institute for Rail Transport. Now she's languishing at some kind of research institute, knitting, reading *Foreign lit*, you know, a sweet, intelligent girl ...

Irka S. will do what she always does at our meetings, she will try not to draw attention to herself, maybe she'll talk about clothes or discos, but we still remember how in tenth grade she would run to the district committee, gathering files and character reports, and, of course, we all know that she's not really studying history, she managed to get into the special program of the law department.

Andryusha, our old *komsorg*,[15] "the most honest and just," will tell a funny story about his learned dog Toby and her incredible puppies.

And I, like always, will smile at everyone and answer: "Great," "Thank you," "I am taking my exams." Everything's fine, fine, fine ...

There are a couple more hours until the meeting. Enough time to distract yourself with your favorite things. My old field of study was medieval history. (The deeper into the past, the better.) Even though the institute spent four years trying to teach me this, I never really learned how to deftly add the requisite spoonful of tar:[16] "The historical limitations of the author were the product of certain social frameworks ..."

I open a little book of medieval poetry. Hundreds of enigmatic sonnets about *La Belle Dame*, "golden-haired, divine, untouchable." Maybe these poets despaired over the terrible gulf between the ideal and the real, the earthly and the divine. Maybe they only dressed up their ambivalence using these familiar, customary forms. Or maybe they did not suffer at all, they merely practiced

---

[15]Komsomol organizer, leader of a unit of the Komsomol, the communist youth party organization for Soviet youth ages fourteeen to twenty-eight.
[16]This references a popular Russian expression: "a spoonful of tar ruins the barrel of honey" ("lozhka dyogtia portit bochku myoda"), whose meaning is similar to the English "fly in the ointment."

belles lettres, wrote programmatic verse, not unlike contemporary production novels. (Today I can't escape this depraved ahistorical approach.) And what about "The Song of Roland?" A wonderful heroic epic or a savage piece of propaganda? It seems to me that it made a significant contribution to the ideological battles of its time, and in this sense is a work worthy of imitation.

"Tu-ru-ru," the radio, as usual, interrupts my train of thought right on time. "Tu-ru-ru-ru. The time in Moscow is 2 o'clock. You are listening to Radio Mayak. The General Secretary of the Central Committee of the Communist Party of the Soviet Union, Chairman of the Presidium of the Supreme Soviet …" The voice is remarkably cheerful and animated. No need to listen any further. You can tell by the timbre and voice modulation what it'll be all about. I've already deduced the pattern: any news broadcast can be divided into three parts.

Part one: "News and visits from socialist countries." Extreme optimism, major key.

Part two: notes of sarcasm, then anger and indignation can be detected. "The American military continues to supply arms to the Republic of South Africa …" "Unemployment reaches record numbers in capitalist countries …" Decline, crisis, fear. But here, too, not all hope is lost: "As the newspaper *Daily World* reports, this week oil refinery workers went on strike …" "English women expressed their support," "a delegation of French schoolteachers is demanding improvements to their workplace environment …"

And finally, part three: "A Hymn to Labor," "In Soviet Lands," "In Preparation for the Nth Congress," "The Labor Watch of the Five-Year Plan," "The collective farm 'Ilyich's way' in the Zhdanov region has committed to …," "Workers at the 'Red Diesel' factory completed ahead of schedule …," "The brigade team contract model is becoming more and more popular …" It all ends on a note of mighty cheer. It's amazing how precisely it is thought out and put together. It is a complete, passionate radio-sonata in three parts: allegro, adagio, allegro molto bravo. At the triumphal sound of the allegro molto bravo I put on my grey coat and white hat and leave the house.

I walk to the subway station. The buildings aren't all that scary in broad daylight. Awkward dirty-white boxes against a grey sky. Not a single bright spot in sight. My grey and white outfit blends into my surroundings. I walk on the wet asphalt; dirt, puddles, and broken branches under my feet.

> we write as we hear
> we hear as we breathe
> I can't shake off these words.

Step. My boot pinches. Step. That damn car really had to splash me. Step … I think I just ran into an old lady carrying a pail. Ding-ding, damn it, watch where you're going! I walk faster. "We write as we hear, we hea …"

Finally, the subway. I press into the crowd, step onto the escalator without thinking, look down. In front of me is a sea of people, all moving chaotically, bumping into each other. In a couple of seconds, I will join them, and the stream will carry me to the platform. I can close my eyes, clear my thoughts, stop worrying; no matter what, sooner or later I will find myself on the train. My empty mind fills with snatches of memorized phrases and poems.

> Tell me, uncle, was there a reason
> that Moscow, burned to the ground,
> was captured by the Freeeeeeeench …[17]
> I know there will be a city,
> I know that gardens will bloom,
> when people like this …[18]

---

[17]Svetlana is here quoting the beginning of Mikhail Lermontov's poem "Borodino," which is about Napoleon's invasion of Russia.
[18]From Mayakovsky's propaganda poem "Khrenov's Story about the Kuznetsk Construction and the People of Kuznetski," this is an oft-quoted optimistic line that was used to motivate workers.

It looks like I am already on the train. There's no place to hide now. Thousands of eyes are fixed on me, measuring me head to toe. Of course, they've noticed the grime on my shoes, the smudged lipstick, the torn glove … No one talks on the subway; the noise of the train absorbs all other sounds. Here you cannot allow yourself the gentle patriarchal sincerity of the tram. Because of this solitude, time slows to a crawl in the tightly packed, brightly lit subway car.

Thank god, this is my stop! But this is not yet the end. I have a transfer ahead of me, another train, a long journey through a maze of underground passages and escalators. I walk alone for a few steps, hide behind an awkward marble column. But the avalanche of people finds me and carries me along, along, along …

I am filled with hate for the girl whose sharp heel just landed on my foot. I shove my elbows hard into the man standing next to me, and the shove is returned with equal force.

All of us comprise one large entity. I no longer have any power over myself. I just need to make sure not to fall behind, I just need to step on the cherished escalator along with everyone else.

I know there will be a city,
I know that gardens will bloooooooooom …

January 23–February 6, 1981.

5

Sasha, Misha, Napoleon and Josephine (circa 1992)

"You are frigid," he told her as they passed by the Gorky monument on Kirov Avenue. She was sorry that he no longer touched her shoulder under the thick wool coat but walked aloof, chewing pink Finnish gum. Frigid – frigidna. Frigida, fetida, femida – she must have been a Roman goddess, with small classical breasts and pupilless eyes of cool marble. It might have been her on that photo in the history textbook, standing side by side with handsome Apollo who had lost his masculine arms. Just before the barbarian invasion … or was it just after? She caught her embarrassed reflection in the window of the Porcelain Shop. It felt uncomfortably damp and raw. She wanted so much to replay the whole scene, to put his hand back under her wool coat, to experience the meaningful weight of his warm finger, to press her cheek against his frosted moustache in that split-second right before they got to the faded neon P of the Porcelain Shop. But it was too late now; he would not give her another chance, another touch. They were already crossing the tram routes and parting by the fence of the park with the poster for Leningrad Dixieland. Season: 1975.

"'Excuse me, miss, are you the last?" "Yes."

"Well, miss … not anymore. Now, I am after you. So, what are we lining up for? What's on offer? Grilled chickens or 'Addresses and Inquiries'?" "Addresses and Inquiries, I hope."

"Good … good … let's hope together. That's the only thing we can do these days – hope. Right? I see you are not from around here …" "No. I am from here …" "Oh yeah? You sure don't look like it … Forgive my curiosity, miss, if you are from around here, why are you lining up at the Information Kiosk?" … "Just looking for my classmates." … "Oh, OK. One has to do that from time to time … I thought you were some kind of foreigner or something …"

Lana realized that she had forgotten how to make small talk in Russian. She had lost that little invisible something that makes you an insider, a tone of voice, a gesture of habitual indifference, half words, half said and fully understood. Lana had emigrated from the Soviet Union eleven years ago: she was told then that it was once and for ever, that there would be no way back for her: it was like life and death. Now she was able to visit Leningrad again. The city had changed its name, and so had she. She came back as an American tourist, rented a room of her own, drank chilled orange juice at the bar in the hotel "Europa," that item of bourgeois charm. She felt guilty and tried to help her Leningrad friends as much as she could. Usually it came our awkwardly; they were too proud to accept her help and she was too direct to know how to give it. Like other idle Westerners, she began to collect Little Octobrist stars representing the baby Lenin with gilded curls, red banners with embroidered golden inscriptions "To the Best Pig Farmer for the Achievement in Labour" or "To the Brigade of a High Level of Culture." Occasionally she wanted to pass for a native here in Leningrad and betrayed herself in passing. Lana (or rather, Svetlana) was born on Bolshoy Avenue, one of the most beautiful avenues in Leningrad. But then again, everyone in Leningrad believed that we lived in the most beautiful city in the world and most likely on the best street, or at least the second best. She lived in Boston on a street with the usual American understated name, Garden Street and then on Prentiss Street. She taught foreign language and literature in the university but she felt more at home, or more "chez soi" in New York City. Could she make small talk in New-Yorkese? Yes, of course. During these years she had learned how to be a foreigner-insider, a foreigner-New-Yorker, together with other resident and non-resident aliens, stateless legal and illegal city dwellers. She was among the lucky green-card carrying New Yorkers and could demonstrate her picture with a properly exposed right ear and a fingerprint. New York was just right. It struck her now that she was much more comfortable in a place like home than at home.

She was a regular at Lox Around the Clock, and could spell her name in two seconds over the phone. Of course, she had an accent, but it was "so very charming", a delicious little extra, like the dressing on a salad that comes free of charge with an order of Manhattan chowder – "'What dressing would you like on your salad, dear?" the waiter would ask her. "Italian, French, Russian or blue cheese?'" "Russian, please," she would say, "and lots of fresh pepper." "What a sweet name you got there, miss. Can you spell it for me?" "Yes, S-like Sam, V-like victory, E-like Ellen, T-like Tom, L-like Larry, A—like Anya …" "All right! Quite a mouthful! Sovetalana?" … "Call me Lana, it's fine."

Besides teaching foreign languages, Lana auditioned to do voiceovers for commercials whenever they needed accents. The last one she did was "La Latta, European youglette, Passion Fat-free – I can't believe it's not yogurt." Female voice: "'Was it Lisboa? Or was Odessa? It was La Latta – like love." "Open your lips, girl, don't be shy. That's not a kiss yet, just a promise of a kiss." Lana loved how casually the word "freedom" was dropped into every commercial like a little protein. Usually what was free was the invisible, that little je-ne sais-quois – forgive my French, that gives everything the right air. She loved her "StayFree" tampons, never choosing "Always" that forever promised more than they could deliver. Of course, if you watch a StayFree commercial you might as well think it's for a vacation spa. Lana imagined a radical ad for her favorite StayFree. A woman artist sitting in her studio in dirty overalls, in the midst of creative disorder. "I will express it," she says with conviction. "I know it's coming. This is going to be my period piece!" She pours scarlet red oil paint into the camera. And again. And again. "StayFree Feminine Pads."

"Are you lining up for inquiries?"

"Yes …"

"And where is the line for addresses?"

"It's here too."

"Well, I actually need a phone number … Of course, it would be great to get a home address too, but I know they're not listed … It's dangerous now … What year is it? 1992! A scary year. It's not like back in the seventies. That was a safe time. Now I don't blame them. What you really need nowadays is an iron door … Don't look at me like that … You think I'm joking … I know you're young, miss, you might think – an iron door, well, that's a bit much … but let me tell you I know a really honest guy, used to be an engineer in the old days … he makes excellent iron doors. Real quality iron. You can call him. Tell him I gave you his number. Tell him, Kolya told me."

"Thanks. I'll think about it …"

"Well, don't think too long or it will be too late … No, of course, spit when you say it. Touch wood. We don't wish anything bad to happen … Maybe there will be law and order in this land one day … or at least order …"

"Hm …"

"Come to think of it, maybe they don't list the phone numbers either. Have you got a pen, miss? Oh, this is such a great pen. What does it say here?"

"Ai LOVE Nyuu York …"

"Did you get it in Gostiny Dvor or in the House of Friendship?"

Lana began to fill out her inquiry cards to avoid further discussion of iron doors. She wanted to find her first teenage loves, Sasha and Misha, with whom she had had her first failed perfect moments. Both relationships had been interrupted. With Sasha, they had split up after this declaration of frigidity and a clumsy wet kiss; with Misha, they had to separate after sealing a secret erotic pact of Napoleonic proportions. She would have liked to update their love stories, to recover a few missing links, to fill in the blanks. They were complete antipodes, Sasha and Misha. Sasha was blond, Misha dark; Sasha was her official story, Misha secretly telephonic; Sasha was beautiful, Misha intellectual. Sasha knew too many girls and Misha had read too much Nietzsche at a young age.

It was almost twenty years ago and the song of the moment was called "First Love." "Oh, the first love, it comes and goes with the tide," sang the Yugoslavian pop star, the beautiful Radmila Karaklajić, blowing kisses out to the sea somewhere near the recently bombed town of Dubrovnik ... In his white coat with blood-red lining, Sasha was beautiful; he had a long black scarf and the aura of a black-market expert. He sang the popular song by Salvatore Adamo about the falling snow: "The snow was falling and you wouldn't come this evening; the snow was falling and everything was white with despair ..." "Tombait la neige ... tu ne viendrais pas ce soir ..." His masculine voice caressed her with the foreign warmth. French snow was falling over and over again, slowly and softly, slowly and softly ... How was it possible that she wouldn't come that evening? Oh, she would, she must come ... and she just couldn't resist. She recalled the shape of his lips, soft, full and cracked, but didn't remember at all what they were talking about. Oh yes, she was a bit taken aback when she found out that he had never read Pasternak. On the other hand, he was a real man and sang beautiful songs. He put his hand under her sweater. He touched her. He tried to unfasten her bra, those silly little hooks on the back, but they just wouldn't yield to him ... "Oh, it doesn't matter. Let me help ..." But he knew that a man must be a man, there are things that a man must do alone ... At that moment a noise in the corridor interrupted them. It was Sasha's father, a former sea captain, coming home after work. The problem was that they did not have anywhere to go: there were no drive-ins, no cars, no back seats available for them; no contraception and only the cheapest Bulgarian wine. Like all Leningrad teenagers they went to walk on the roofs of the Peter and Paul Fortress. That was a minor transgression. They walked right under the sign "No dogs allowed. Walking on the roofs is strictly prohibited ..." They would get all icy and slippery and one could easily slip, distracted by the gorgeous panorama of the Neva embankment. But it was quite spectacular, the imperial palace dissolving in the mist, dark grey ripples on the river, a poem or two ... Wait, do you remember how it goes ... ? "Life is a lie, but with a charming sorrow ..." "Yes," she would say, "yes" ... But that day they parted before the entrance to the park. On the way she worried that her nose was becoming frozen red and that she didn't look good any more. She was too embarrassed to look at him and could only catch glimpses of his blond curls, his scarf and the dark birthmark on his cheek. Then there were some clumsy gestures and an unexpected wetness on her lips. Did I kiss him or not? She tried to concentrate because this was supposed to be her perfect moment.

"You are frigid," he said very seriously. Frigid ... frigid ... a blushing goddess. So, that's what it was called? This clumsiness, arousal, alienation, excitement, tongue-tiedness, humidity, humility, humiliation.

"Are you waiting for apricot juice?"

"No ..."

"You mean the apricot juice is gone? I don't believe it ... this is really incredible ... All they got is the Scottish Whisky."

"'Miss, where are you from?"

This time Lana did not protest. She began to fill in Misha's card – all in red ink. Misha did not know French songs and did not care much about Salvatore Adamo. They spoke only about Nietzsche, orgasms and the will to power. "Orgasms: they must be simultaneous or nothing at all. They are beyond good and evil ... For protection women could simply put a little piece of lemon inside them. It's the most natural method, practiced by poets during the Silver Age ..." If her relationship with Sasha was a conventional romance with indispensable walks on the roofs of the fortress, her relationship with Misha was an example of teenage nonconformism. They dated mostly on the phone and saw each other only about three times during their two-year ongoing erotic conversation. She could still hear his familiar voice, which had already lost its high boyish pitch and acquired a deep guttural masculinity, resounding in her right ear. When she thought about Misha, she saw herself sitting in a clumsy pose on an uncomfortable chair near the "communal" telephone, counting the black squares on the tiled checkered floor. The telephone was placed in the corridor and shared by all the neighbors of the apartment. While talking to Misha she had to lower her voice, because her neighbor Shura, the voracious gossiper, was conspicuously going back and forth between her room and the kitchen, slowing her steps near the phone. The rest of the time she was probably standing behind the doors of her room, busy filling in the gaps in Lana and Misha's fragmented dialogue. With Misha she was very intimate but their intimacy was safe, and the distance protected them from self-censorship. They knew that they were partaking in a larger system of official public communication. The invisible presence of the others, the flutter of slippers in the corridor, pleasantly tickled their nerves. Lana met Misha on the Devil's Wheel – a special whirligig in the Kirov Park of Culture and Leisure. Misha fell victim to the calumny of Lana's girlfriend, Ira, who observed his immediate affection for Lana. "He's handsome," Ira said, "but he has smooth rosy cheeks ... like a girl ... you know what I mean ..." "He has smooth rosy cheeks like a girl ..." – this strange sentence haunted Lana for the whole day, that beautiful spring day when they were riding on the whirligig trying to touch each other in the air in a moment of ephemeral intimacy, and then push each other away, swinging on the chains. The song goes like this:

Just remember long ago in the spring, we were riding in the park on Devil's Wheel. Devil's Wheel, Devil's Wheel and your face is flying near me. But I am swinging on the chains, I am flying – OH!

"Oh?" "I am swinging on the chains. I am flying." "Akh, Akh."

"I thought you were humming the old song 'Devil's Wheel.' Haven't heard it on the radio for ages ... It must be ten years old ..."

"Yeah ... I don't know why it stuck with me."

"It's a nice song. I remember our great talent Muslim Magomaev used to sing it on the TV on New Year's Eve. It was when I was still married to my ex-wife and our son was in the army ... She would be making her New Year potato salad in the kitchen with my mother-in-law and I would watch TV, that show called 'Little Blue Light.' And then there would be a clock and the voice of comrade Brezhnev – first it was comrade Brezhnev himself, then his voice, and in the last years the voice of an anchorman reading Brezhnev's speech – poor guy had a tic – but the speech always sounded so warm and familiar and it went so well with a little glass of vodka and herring: 'Dear Soviet citizens ... The coming year promises us further achievements on our victorious road to Communism ... I wish you good health, happiness in your personal life and success in your labour.' And then Muslim Magomaev would sing 'Devil's Wheel':

Just remember long ago in the spring, we were riding in the park on Devil's Wheel. Devil's Wheel, Devil's Wheel ..."

"I know these days you're not supposed to remember things like that ... Now it's called 'the era of stagnation ... '"

"But it was such a good song ..."

Lana was afraid to lose Misha's face forever at the next turn of the whirligig. "Devil's Wheel, Devil's Wheel, and your face is flying near me." The words of this popular song shaped their romance. But in this whirlpool of excitement, in the swings of the Devil's Wheel, in the cool air of a Russian spring, his cheeks were getting rosier and rosier. The obscene words froze on the tip of her tongue. He blushed like a girl. They were doomed ... They would have been a strange couple anyway – his girlish rosy cheeks and deep masculine voice, and her boyish clumsiness and long red nails painted with an imported Polish nail polish. They didn't know what to do with their excessively erotic and intellectual selves.

After the encounter on the Devil's Wheel there were months of phone calls. They carefully planned their next meeting and always postponed it. Finally, they decided, now or never, they would conduct a secret ritual, the deepest penetration into the mysteries of the soul. She left her house and walked away from the city centre. She passed the larger-than-life portrait of Lenin made of red fishnet in the 1960s. Behind the monument to the Russian inventor of radio, Alexander Popov, there was urban no man's land, the old botanical gardens with ruined greeneries, endless fences made of wood and iron. This was the border zone – exactly what Misha looked for to perform their secret ritual. "This could be done once in a lifetime," he said seriously. "Napoleon did it to Josephine." She had to stand against the iron fence with her hands behind her back and open her eyes very wide. Then he touched her eye with his tongue. He touched it deeply, trying to penetrate into the darkness of the pupil. For a second, he lingered, and then licked the white around her eyelids as if drawing the contours of her vision from inside her. Her gaze acquired primordial warmth and humidity. They paused for a moment. Her eyes were overflowing with desire. They never condescended to kissing, holding each other, or saying a romantic "I love you" on the roof of the fortress. They despised these conventional teenage games. They committed a single Napoleonic transgression, a moment of dazzling eye contact, a mysterious pact of intimacy signed with neither ink nor blood.

"Miss, you'll have to rewrite this ... We do not accept red ink. And the paper is wet. Try to be neat ..."

"Forgive me. I have terrible handwriting ..."

"That's your problem. And hurry please, we close in an hour ..."

"But we've been waiting an hour and a half."

"Well, yesterday, people stood for three hours under drizzling rain. Be grateful that you're queuing for information, not for bread ..."

"Oh, by the way, speaking of bread, you should have seen what they sell in the cooperative bakery around the corner. Their heart-shaped sweet breads are now five hundred roubles apiece ... I mean this is ridiculous ... They used to be twenty kopecks – maximum."

"What are you talking about? We didn't even have heart-shaped breads before ... If it were up to you and people like you, we would still live in the era of stagnation or, even worse, in the time of the great purges ... You just can't take any change ..."

"Hey, comrades, ladies and gentlemen, whatever ... Stop yelling in line. These working conditions are impossible! I can't give out any information with all of this shouting!"

And in New York there are a hundred kinds of breads – Lana suddenly felt ashamed of it – bread with and without calories, with and without fat, bread which is not really bread at all, but only looks like it. This bread will never get stale; it is non-perishable, eternally fresh and barely edible. So sometimes you have to rush to an expensive store, miles away to fetch foreign bread that lasts only for a day, that is fattening and crusty and doesn't fit in the toaster. So, she did not express her views on the heart-shaped cakes. She tried hard to remain neutral and friendly with all the strangers in the line and concentrated on filling out her inquiry cards. But those two repulsively intimate episodes were her main clues for Sasha and Misha. The rest was the hearsay of well-meaning common friends, rumors, and most of them fifteen years old.

Sasha, rumor had it, was married and drinking. Or rather, at the beginning he did everything right – he flirted with the black market in his early youth, but then cut off all his blond curls and ties with foreigners and entered the Military Naval Academy. He married his high-school sweetheart, whom he had begun to date in the resort town of Z just about the time of their romance, and who had heroically waited for him through all those years. Of course, they had a very proper wedding in the Palace of Weddings on the Neva embankment and they placed the crown of flowers in the Revolutionary Cemetery and took lots of pictures with her white lacy veil and his black tuxedo. Sasha wanted to be a noble army officer, like his father, a youngish-looking, well-built man, who often played tennis at the courts of the town of Z. He was the "right stuff." But then something unforeseen occurred. Sometime in the early 1980s he started to develop strange symptoms, losing hair and getting a dark rash on his arms. Nobody was sure what it was. During his service somewhere in the Arctic

Circle, Sasha might have received an excessive dose of radiation. But those were the things that one didn't talk about, you know what I mean ... He quit the service, left the city and underwent special medical treatment somewhere far away. He came back supposedly cured. Is one ever? Lana's distant cousin, Sasha's occasional tennis partner, said that he was in Leningrad, but that he had moved from his old apartment and no longer spent summers in the town of Z. Another common friend had spotted him in the subway passage, but Sasha didn't say hello. Was he preparing for a new diplomatic career? Secret service? Private securities? The crowd was moving fast, the light was dim, and, who knows, it might have been someone else altogether ...

As for Misha, he was considered lucky. Like Sasha, he did not keep in touch with old friends, but then again, those old friends did not keep in touch with each other, just gathered occasionally, for someone's birthday or a farewell party. Misha started as unconventionally as one would expect of him. In the late 1970s he managed to get into the philosophy department, which was an almost impossible thing to do without connections. He had to settle for the evening division, in which case he had to serve time in the Soviet army. What might have seemed like a tragedy turned out to have a peculiar "happy ending". Misha spent two years in the Far East, in the most dangerous area, near the Chinese border. He told her during one of their last long conversations after he returned from the army that in his detachment, he was the only person with a high-school education. So, he could satisfy his will to power. The soldiers polished his boots, squatted in front of him and methodically brushed away every tiny bit of dust. He liked it. He said that of all things in the world, he loved power the most. Lana thought that he must have still been into Nietzsche.

By the age of twenty-one he was chosen to enter the Communist Party on a special basis, two years before the official age of eligibility, which was twenty-three. During the 1980 Russian Olympic Games – the last epic event of the Brezhnev era – Misha was elected to the Leningrad Olympic Committee. He called her then, appearing very friendly, and promised to get her some Ceylon tea which had long vanished from the stores and could only be acquired by the privileged few. She couldn't forgive him for this tea for a long time. Perhaps it was not the tea itself but a certain tone of voice … That year she became something like an internal refugee and had to leave the university, "expelled voluntarily." She applied for emigration and soon after that friends stopped visiting her. Occasionally they called from public phones and spoke in strange voices, and then, when something squeaked in the receiver, quickly bid their farewells: "Forgive me, I am out of change. I'll call you later." Lana was running endless errands, as a therapy against fear, collecting the "inquiry cards and papers" – *spravki* – to and from various departments of Internal Affairs … And yes, good tea was really hard to get in those days, especially the sweet and aromatically prestigious Ceylon tea.

She often imagined meeting Misha somewhere in the noisy subway, in the midst of a crowd. He would proudly wear his great tan and fashionable brand-new T-shirt with the winking Olympic bear, made in Finland. "I've been transferred to Moscow you know," he shouted at her. "I've been very busy lately." "Me too," Lana shouted in response. "I am emigrating, you know." She knew she was compromising him at that moment, that she was saying something that one did not talk about, something that one could only whisper in private and never on the phone. A few strangers conspicuously turned around to look at them as if photographing Misha's face and hers with their suspicious eyes. And then Misha blushed, in his unique girlish fashion, his cheeks turned embarrassingly red, as in those teenage years, and he vanished in the crowd. But all of this took place many years ago, and Lana no longer had any problems with tea. Those fragments of intimacy with Misha and Sasha, tactile embarrassments and unfulfilled desires, were the few things that remained vivid in her mind from the "era of stagnation." Those incomplete narratives and failed perfect moments were like fragile wooden logs, unreliable safeguards on the swamp of her Leningradian memory that otherwise consisted of inarticulate fluttering and stutters, smells and blurs.

Lana had already performed some of the obligatory homecoming rituals, but they were too literal and therefore disappointing. She walked by the ageing but still cheerful Gorky on the renamed Kirov Avenue, approaching the windows of the Porcelain Store, which now sold all possible commercial goods from chicken grills to Scottish Whisky and Wrangler jeans. Across the street from the square with the monument to the Russian inventor of radio (whose invention, among many other things, is now called into question) she searched in vain for the red shadow of Lenin made of fishnet. The house where she used to live was being repaired and on the broken glass door of the gala entrance, she found a poster advertising a popular Mexican soap opera, "And the Rich Also Cry." Otherwise the façade looked exactly as in the old days, but it appeared more like an impostor for her old house, or a stage set that clumsily imitated the original. Lana climbed up to their communal apartment through piles of trash. The place looked uncanny. The old communal partitions, including the secret retreats of the neighbor Aunt Shura who bore witness to her teenage romances, were taken apart and the whole drama of communal life was forever interrupted. On the floor she found broken telephone wires, worn-out slippers and pieces of a French record. She looked through the window: black bottomless balconies were still precariously attached to the building and a few rootless plants continued to inhabit them. A melancholy lonely drunk urinated near the skeleton of the old staircase.

"Comrades, Ladies and Gentlemen. Remember who is the last in line and no more lining up after that. Can I trust you?"

"But of course, we are all family here, miss. We know who stood in line and who didn't."

"Hurry up, comrades. Prepare your inquiry cards neatly. Be sure to include name and patronymic, place of birth, nationality, permanent address ... We are short of time here ..."

Indeed, we are short of time, thought Lana. We are all only a phone call away from each other. Misha, Sasha, let's all get together. Let bygones be bygones – God, we used to learn so many proverbs in our English classes and then never had occasion to use them … Let's chat, remember the golden seventies, have a drink or two. What do you think? There are so many blank spots in our life stories, and we don't have to fill them all, it's OK. We'll just have fun. Let's meet in some beautiful spot with a view, definitely with a view. We don't need broad panoramas, no. And I don't think the Temple of our Savior in Blood is such a good place. (I heard they took the scaffolding down and you can actually see it now; it's been restored after so many years …) Let's meet on the little bridge with golden-winged lions. "Let's tell each other compliments, in love's special moments." I didn't make up this song; it really existed. Take it easy, Sasha … I know what happened. I've heard. I don't have much to say about it, only that it could have been worse. Listen, you looked really gorgeous in that white coat with red lining and I was completely and totally seduced by that silly song … I must have had a real crush on you. I even forgave you for not reading Pasternak. It's just that we took ourselves so seriously in those days, you and me … But tell me, where did you get that cruel Latin word "frigid" from? In America, you know, women are rarely frigid, but the weather frequently is … Hey, Misha. I've really forgotten about that Ceylon tea of yours … it doesn't matter anymore; I've brought you some Earl Grey … Remember our telephonic orgasms in the communal corridor? God, I wish someone had taped those … Should we try to continue in a more sedate grown-up fashion and shock the long-distance operator? I think I know something about you from the time your army boots were still unpolished. The taste of your tongue in my eyes … Where are you now? Way up or low down? As usual, beyond good and evil? I am joking, of course; you might have forgotten your high-school Nietzsche … Me, I'm fine really. I love New York, as they say. Like New Yorkers, love it and hate it. It feels like home and I feel a bit homesick now, for that little studio of mine on the Ninth West Street, bright but rather messy, without pretense of coziness.

Sometimes I go traveling to the end of the world, or at least to the southernmost point in the United States. Last time I nearly slipped on the wet rocks. You see, you need that, to get a perspective, to estrange yourself. It's dangerous to get attached to one place, don't you think? And yes, of course I must be having great sex. For that's what we do "in the West" and it couldn't be otherwise. It's not so simple. Physically we know much more about each other, you know, we talk and we name things. But my new boyfriend says that he hasn't found himself yet. (Found whom, you would ask ...) I know it might sound funny here, some people try to lose themselves and others to find ... Well ... let's have a cup of coffee.

Where shall we sit? You are local, you must know places. Yesterday we tried to have a drink with my old girlfriend and we couldn't find a place to sit. It was raining. So, we ended up in the movie theatre, The Barricade, on Nevsky. They have a nice coffee shop. We even bought the ticket to the movies, just in case. They were showing *Crocodile Dundee*. The cleaning woman tried to get us to go to see the movie.

"Hey, kids. Oh, it's such a funny movie," she said. "You just can't stop laughing. Our movies are never funny like that."

"No," I said, "we paid for the ticket but really we just want to sit in the coffee shop since it's open till the next show."

"But – it can't be done," she said, "'the coffee shop is for moviegoers only and what kind of moviegoers are you?"

"We are ticket-holders. Besides, I have already seen *Crocodile Dundee*," I protested.

"It's impossible ... Don't try to fool me. This is the first night ..."

"I saw it in the drive-in in New London," I insisted ...

"Look, miss, leave the coffee shop this very minute. I tell you that in Russian, loud and clear. Coffee is for moviegoers only."

Maybe we'll see a movie, Misha, something very slow, with long, long takes. Wait, Misha, don't rush ... I am sure we'll find a place nearby ... I would have invited you for a bagel, but it's far away … We could talk about Napoleon. He is sort of out of fashion now … I bet the waitress would take us for ageing foreign students …"

"The information kiosk closes in fifteen minutes."

"Wait, dear miss, you've promised us so much … we've waited for so long …"

"This is public abuse. I demand the 'Book of Complaints and Suggestions' …"

"I am sorry, comrade, we don't have it at this branch of the Information Kiosks. You would have to go to the Central Information Bureau on Nevsky Avenue. But they close at two today, so you are too late. And tomorrow they have a day off."

"That's the whole problem … Whatever the reason, Russian people love to complain … I would have prohibited those 'Books of Complaints and Suggestions' … What we need is 'The Book of Constructive Proposals.'"

"And who are you, mister? Are you a people's deputy, or what?"

"No, I am not."

"Well, we are very glad that you are not the people's deputy. People have a right to information. If they can't get the information, they can complain … We've been silenced for too long …"

"So what? Before we didn't have any information, now it's all over the place … But who needs it when we can't afford toothpaste! We don't have toothpaste, but we've got glasnost to freshen our breath … Information … If you want my opinion, there is too much information these days, too much talk and no change …"

"Excuse me," she said very politely. "It is written here clearly: "The Information Kiosk is open from 11 a.m. to 5 p.m., Monday through Thursday."

"Today is Thursday and it is quarter to four now, therefore the kiosk should be open for another hour and fifteen minutes."

"Hey, lady ... and who do you think I am? Do you think I can't read or something? You try working here for a fucking hundred roubles per hour. I would be making twice as much in the cooperative bakery ... But I stay here all the same. I feel sorry for folks like you, filling out those fucking inquiry cards in the cold ... Someone has to give people the information they need ..."

"Excuse me, miss ... Where are you from?"

6

Replace the Irreplaceable! A Tale of Immigrant Objects

The original Royal Heirloom Victoria & Albert cup was purchased in a warehouse in Collinsville, Connecticut that no longer exists. I remember that it was the only cup on the shelf that didn't have the label "like new." The cup contained fine crazings in its glaze, and a brown stain, a memory of past tea drinkers. "Authentic," said the salesman. "Made of pulverized bone ashes. Somebody's grandma loved it." I knew it wasn't my grandma but it didn't really matter.

Since my immigration from Leningrad to Boston, I had developed a fondness for the American flea markets, yard sales and free antiques that appear miraculously on city streets on trash days. Too poor to shop for household goods, we used to look for treasures from trash; coffee tables with missing curved legs and incrustations, vanity cabinets with broken mirrors, clocks with missing hands, how-to-change-your-life books and pieces of non-pareil bone china. Trash hunting was a form of our subsistent living. It was fun too. We repurposed other people's souvenirs and made them our own. "The crazing on this cup goes rather deep," I told the salesman. "Can I get a discount?" "No," he said. "This is the final sale." On the day I broke the cup I had my own fine crazing, fractured tibia and fibula bones and a broken marriage. I had to learn how to hobble around my house on one leg to avoid a repeat injury. When our bones are intact, we walk the way we breathe – thoughtlessly. We trust our feet to uproot us gently and land us safely in the near abroad. But now everything was shaky again. The second home that I made for myself in Boston didn't feel like home anymore. It became a maze of displaced objects, souvenirs of past lives, gifts from forgotten friends, extension cords connected to nothing, book pages with sharp edges that make your fingers bleed. Hopping in the slip-proof sock, the color of hospital beige, I felt I was on a domestic reconnaissance mission. I touched every threshold, every deviant nail, every gap in the wooden boards of the floor. The skeleton of my house revealed itself to me. I crisscrossed its history like an obstacle course.

This fateful morning, I just want to have a good time. To drink some strong tea with lemon from my heirloom cup without anyone's help. I am sick and tired of my step-by-step existence and of starting every morning with "rating my pain on a scale of one to ten" in "My Diary of Pain" that the hospital nurse left for me. In general, following instructions is not my strong point. How to move objects in space, how to scratch the itch, how to lead a risk-averse life without bending your knee. I like making my own rules. For example: How to give a kiss on crutches. Follow three simple steps. Identify a body part of the individual you intend to kiss and not an arbitrary moving target. Hug the crutch with your armpit, lean forward with your upper body and extend your neck. Just tenderness, no obligation. Make sure you don't hit the funny bone. If there is no human in sight, just kiss your bone china and take a long sip. So, I climb on top of my mobile bed, stand on one leg, open the door of the glass cabinet with the help of my crutch and barely holding onto the shelf, grab the handle of my favorite tea cup. I put myself in harm's way and take the risk for its own sake. Mission accomplished! My Heirloom Victoria & Albert cup is safe in my hands. I move to the kitchen, carrying the cup in one hand, jumping on one leg and passing containers from one surface to another. I do it with the dexterity of an experienced cast member, relishing my new self-sufficiency. I hold the cup by its elegant handle, bring the gilded rim to my lips and drink slowly. It's pleasant to kill time, something I can't afford to do when I stand on my own two feet. At that nearly perfect moment the phone rings. I leap to answer it, to respond, to bear weight, just like in the good old days. My hand grasps for help, my elbow hits the cup and I watch it fall and break into large shards, as if in slow motion. I know better than to leap to its rescue. The remains of the heirloom are scattered on the black and white chessboard of the linoleum floor. I cannot lean down to gather them. The only thing I can do is to flee the wreckage with caution and care. It has to be left as it is. There is no way for me to remove the traces. I cannot even bend my knee. Until the first visitor comes, I will have to live next to the scene of the accident, the pieces of bone china teasing me with their rough edges. But don't worry about me. I don't break down. What scares me is how quickly I turn my back on grief. I have learnt to break things. I have mastered the art of losing.

What's lost is lost. A cup is only a cup. I hold onto its gilded handle, ever more beautiful when attached to nothing.

A few hours pass eventless. Evening descends with a flash of twilight blue, the color of the East German Kodak film of my childhood. There is a knock at my kitchen door. I forgot completely about the visit of my colleague. M. was supposed to deliver the files from a recent department meeting. M. is sympathetic, but also very professional. I wonder for a moment what to do about my mess. He is not obliged to bear witness to any of it. Should I laugh it off or gently ask if he could sweep the pieces into the dustbin because I cannot do it on my own? But then I would have to go into embarrassing details about my bones, which only the injured could relate to. Will he think it too intimate? Will it tamper with the New England sense of boundaries which makes our relationship so comfortable? If he was Russian, I would ask, but he is not. Besides, he lost his partner not too long ago; so he might be in mourning. And he is, most certainly, short on time. M. greets me with warm politeness. I don't draw his attention to what is blatantly in front of him, and he makes no mention of it. He walks through my barricaded kitchen and we proceed directly to work. We have a nice talk. He apologizes that he came with nothing: "empty-handed, as you would say in Russian." On his way out, he walks around the broken shards like a weathered journalist through ruins and warzones, either oblivious of them or too mindful. I can't tell. With nothing better to do I am left to compose a requiem for the broken bone china.

 One day in the middle of nowhere central Connecticut we stopped by an old mill factory turned antique warehouse, itself part ruin, part construction site. The visit was short because we wanted to make it home before dark. The reticent New England sun was ready to retreat away from public view. Most of the store's displays were already in boxes and the place gave the impression of a transit station where immigrants sorted their personal belongings. I wandered through the rows of dispersed silver sets, oversized fur coats with ripped buttons, catching my disheveled reflection in yet another vanity cabinet straight out of a 1950s B-movie. Suddenly a single tea cup caught my attention. It was not part of any set. It stood alone. Dark blue and gold with rose bouquets in deep pink, the color of nostalgia itself. A belated Victorian craze, the Queen mourning the love of her life, pressing her lips to the tender rim. Fortified by pulverized bone ashes? No, that's not it. I see instead my no less virginal Aunt Mirrah in a dark blouse: her first barely kissed love died in the battle of Stalingrad. A tentative kiss on a stairwell, a friendly postcard, a light blush upon being discovered by a curious neighbor. Whatever it had or hadn't been we would never find out. After the war many women in my family were widowed or unmarried. Aunt Mirrah lived with Aunt Berta in a meticulously dusted semi-dark room stuffed with porcelain figurines of bare-chested shepherdesses and their rosy-cheeked companions who blew hot air into tibia-shaped flutes. Glass cabinets stood against the wall filled with mementos of dispersed tea sets. (Don't play with the key, children!) And there it was: Royal Heirloom Victoria & Albert cup or its perfect imitation. Aunt Mirrah derived an almost erotic pleasure from reaching into the cabinet's dark corners, outwitting the patina of time. The sparkling clean china cabinet reflected in the double mirror gave the crammed room an illusion of depth.

Such cabinets, filled with odd collections of cups, toys and souvenirs from the places never visited, could be found in many postwar Soviet apartments. Most of these apartments in the center of Leningrad were communal; behind the gorgeous urban façades decorated with masks, exotic beasts, and columns of all possible orders, were dark courtyards, back staircases, and dimly lit partitioned flats crumbling from disrepair. The long corridors leading to the shared kitchen and toilet were painted with a thin blue line below waist level and decorated with endless lists of instructions and rules regulating communal behavior. But the rooms opened into a different cozy world with a small oasis of beauty, a private corner of the communal apartment with smelly toilets and no shower. The cabinet of ordinary curiosities was an altar to personal dreams from another age, neither properly Soviet nor consumerist.

The variety of objects was limited and predictable, and only the web of family storytelling made those similar displays singular and unique. I might be the last clumsy storyteller from the displaced dynasty, "differently abled," as they say in America. I know history from hearsay and books. I only imagine what historical and personal upheavals these objects have witnessed. In the late 1920s there was a campaign against "domestic trash" that promoted the purge of foreign objects, including evil porcelain figurines of class enemies, excessively decorative china cups, potted fichus plants that carried the seeds of bourgeois hominess and the cagey and counter-revolutionary yellow canaries which the Soviet poet Mayakovsly proposed to strangle, at least poetically if not literally. "Quickly, comrades, twist the throats of the yellow canaries before they twist the throat of communism," he wrote in the poem "On Trash." Yet during the major revolutionary transformation of the country from Lenin's to Stalin's times, most Soviet citizens lived with the private things from another time, oddly outmoded and eccentric. How they survived dispossessions, revolutions, relocations and then World War II and the siege of Leningrad,

I have no idea. During the siege, Aunt Mirrah must have hidden them somewhere safe, nobody remembers where. She poured the remainder of her love into them, swaddling them in warm cloth. The survival of Aunt Mirrah's heirloom cup was a miracle of courage and contingency. I remember how this precariously glued treasure wobbled in the chest of drawers when we kids played our irreverent hide-and-seek. What do you prefer, hiding or seeking? Of course, I want to hide, to make myself invisible and immobile and watch how the world can exist without me. How silly my friend looks searching for me under the orange sofa bed. I have tricked everyone. Oh no! Now she's going to the coat closet! I hid there a week ago; what is she thinking? How I laughed silently at the blindness of the seekers. Now I know that I liked to hide because I never doubted that I would be found or at least that there would be someone looking for me. You hide to be sought after. I played out my own disappearance, but played it safe. And once found, I would jump with joy, causing the precious altar to jiggle. "Hey, careful! Don't jump around. Remember the cups!" Kind Aunt Mirrah tutored me in math and offered me tea when I found the correct solution to a difficult puzzle. Obviously, we wouldn't even dream of drinking from the precious cup; we would only admire it from afar. The tea was offered in a simple Soviet cup with gilded red roosters. As the weak tea was getting lukewarm in my Soviet cup, the heirloom roses on the Royal Albert exuded the delicate aroma of an elegant past – not my aunt's but someone else's, which she had accidentally inherited.

Somehow, in my family, the stories of cherished and lost objects are better preserved than the stories of people's lives. We spoke more about our apartment interiors than about our interior lives. Psychotherapy was part of the state security apparatus. My mother once said that what mattered was just to have food and drink on the table, to be together and not to dig too deeply into the past. She didn't believe in complaining or in breaking down, mentally or physically. Crazing was not for her. She simply couldn't afford it. My grandmother had an old feud with Aunt Mirrah and it was all about bone china, not about the cruel fates of its owners – nobody wanted to touch on that. Most members of their large family died young – from mass executions, wars and disease. All that remained were old photographs in exotic costumes, porcelain figurines, heirloom cups and tall blue vases, possibly made in Limoges. My grandmother was arrested as a "rootless cosmopolitan" and sent to the camps in 1949; when she came back in 1955, she was amazed to find that her carefully hidden bone china and the vases survived her imprisonment. Nobody was particularly interested to hear her story from the Gulag at that time, but everyone talked about the enduring things. During the Khrushchev Thaw of the 1960s my young parents fought their own campaign against "domestic trash." They wanted to live in a new way, with uncluttered rooms and without the burden of the past. The old-fashioned tea set and vases were sent into fashion exile and were relocated to the closet of our communal apartment. I grew up with cheerful tea ware decorated with golden cocks and yellow wallpaper with dandelions brightly illuminated by large red lampshades – made in Yugoslavia or Czechoslovakia – that looked like friendly UFOs. The old things became valuable again when I decided to emigrate at the age of twenty, looking for my own new life elsewhere beyond the stifling familiarity of the communal apartments.

My parents had to come up with the money to pay endless bribes and fees to make my emigration possible. My grandmother's vases were sold for cheap, there was no time to bargain, timing was everything. I emigrated back in the 1980s, before perestroika. At that time, I could take hardly any valuables with me, just one suitcase and ninety dollars per person. I was young and didn't care too much about things. At the last moment my mother packed my cup with the golden rooster because she had heard that everybody drinks from paper cups in faraway America. Not so precious in my Russian life, the cup became a priceless memento of emigration. When one moves from a land of planned scarcity to a land of planned obsolescence, it is hard to preserve one's habits and frames of mind. Perhaps that's why in America the frames are often more valuable than the artwork. Frames are nailed to the walls of your home; pictures are transitory and portable. People say that I did well on the whole, I learned a new language and shortened my sentences. I married an American man and tried to build a second home. I assimilated. I bought glass cabinets of my own and some bric-a-brac in a vintage store called "History" on Massachusetts Avenue that recently went out of business. My ex-husband, a pacifist, collected toy soldiers from another time and constantly fought imaginary battles. I assembled my own ragtag army of Russian clay heroes, troikas, fat Madonnas, centaurs with balalaikas and magic birds with whistles under their tails. I bought new replicas of Russian imperial china cups, the "cobalt net."

Unlike my careful aunts, I used my precious teacup all the time, saving it neither for a rainy day nor for a bright future. In our family history the bone china proved to be more resilient than its owners. Aunt Mirrah was right; the young generation never learnt how to handle things with care. One day I broke my old cup with the golden cock that I carried with me in my one immigrant bag. To tell you the truth, I didn't throw it in the trash. I planned to many times, but I didn't. I may have put the shard with the beheaded red rooster into some immigrant closet. Don't get me wrong. Mostly I take out my trash on schedule and even recycle. But sometimes it's hard to part with a beautiful piece, so I keep it in the limbo of my closet, between archive and garbage. But where is this story going? There is no all-purpose glue that would put these broken shards together again. Now that my former home country has broken apart, for better and for worse, and my grandmother and Aunt Mirrah are no more, who cares about those orphaned things? It was worth it for me to lose them, right? I'm glad I left and traveled light. With lightness came liberty. Once you leave home, the other losses matter less. The shock of finitude hurts at first and then becomes habitual. It's like a blood test. "Just a pinch," says the nurse. "Sorry, have to pinch again … Your veins are so thin. Make a fist. Deep breathe. Look away. OK. One more pinch, honey. Your blood's moving slowly, but we're getting there ..." Bloodletting makes you a little light-headed. Lying in the middle of domestic ruin I am reminded of my missed mourning.

Ruin means "collapse," but it is also about remainders and reminders, about past dreams of the future and alternative veins of history. The laughing masks on the cracked façade of my Leningrad house, built by a foreign architect, smile at me. I remember dandelions on the yellow wallpaper, the torn-up pages of the *Pravda* newspaper circa 1974 in our unheated communal toilet, a mist of Red Moscow Eau de Cologne in the lobby to cover up the smell. We are dipping Mashenka cookies in weak tea, laughing at the same joke with a scratchy French record playing in the background. "Tombait la neige. Tu ne vendrais pas ce soir ..." I don't recall exactly who "we" are but we all feel at home. Only it's not what you think. I really don't want to go back there. I have no plans to recover the unreal estate. I'd like to hobble forward into the crutchless future, to move on, to find another country to emigrate to, the way I have all my life. Instead I trip. I stumble into something I was blind to. I may not miss lost objects, but I miss telling stories about them. I miss having someone to tell stories to about lost objects. Do you hear me? Is that too much to ask?

Meander back to the beginning. To a factory town in Connecticut, not to Leningrad. I am browsing again through the displaced domestic things in the warehouse when I realize I'm not alone there. I am with you, of course, my American ex-husband. You've been hiding there in the background of my story, or rather you haven't been hiding at all, just waiting for me in the car, impatient with my erring and wandering, but also giving me time. Of course, we were together then. We went to visit your relatives in Connecticut, and this trip to the antique store was my little reward for all the uncomfortable silences and tensions that we'd been through. We felt safe together, you and I, maybe not intimate but homey. We didn't question that, just played our comforting hide-and-seek with a little jazz in the background. We didn't confront difficult things and spoke with half-words, the way I'd been used to in my Soviet past. My second home had a few dimly lit corners like my first one. Your Napoleonic toy soldiers peacefully coexisted with my Russian dolls. All passions and power struggles were ancient history. You never liked tea but I could still tell you my stories whether you listened or not. You looked at my heirloom cup with a mixture of indifference and tenderness and said something unmemorable like, "It's nice. Almost new." Now I am breaking down. No place to hide in this mess. Too much wear and tear everywhere. The room hasn't been aired for ages. Quickly, I have to move sideways, take another path in my story, a road not taken. Go back to Aunt Mirrah's shadowy room, follow her first love, the one-legged lieutenant with a husky voice and smoky breath. What if he comes back from the war with a medal, rings the bell twice, as usual, and the wise Aunt Mirrah wearing a crepe de chine dress with curlers in her hair forgives him his fleeting wartime infidelities? And the heirloom cups jiggle behind the squeaky-clean glass happily ever after. The phone rings. I pick up carefully without rushing. It's my friend Kati. She knows that something is not right from the slight quiver in my voice. "Come on." she says. "Sometimes, a cup is just a cup. It's not even yours."

"No," I say sobbing. "It's not just a cup. This one had a story behind it." "OK," says Kati matter-of-factly. "Let's see. Have you tried www.replacetheirreplacable.com?" In haste, I google the "Prince Albert Heirloom Cup." I am redirected from one homepage to another. I drag the arrow impatiently past the endless Wedgewood landscapes of the English picturesque, past the Japanese cherry blossoms and the golden dandelions on the imperial Russian cobalt, circa 2013. Finally, here it is. My cup's fair sibling with photoshopped highlights. The bouquet is slightly different, but you know, a rose is a rose. This cup is "like new" with a few cracks and identity marks. I am in a rush. I part, without hesitation, with my personal information, leave my credit card number, security code, my address, phone number, my mother's maiden name. Who cares about identity theft when you can replace the irreplaceable? Which cup am I replacing? My aunt's, or my own? Don't distract me. I have no time to care – my online bid is desperately time-sensitive. I'm gambling on recovery. This cup will be mine, like new, with pulverized bone ashes, crazings and flowers in bloom.

7

My Significant Others: Zenita, Susana, Ilanka

On the day of my birth my father was at a football match. The Kirov stadium was decorated with red banners soaked in Leningrad drizzle: "Forward, to the Victory of Communism!" and my father's favorite team, Zenit of Leningrad, were losing as usual. That did not upset my father in the very least. He was an honorary member of the Club of Fervent Fans of Zenit (KZBZ in Russian), whose task it was simply to bet on Zenit's chances of victory or defeat. What mattered for the fervent fans was the game itself and the community of friends that created their own state within a state to share a few permissible laughs.

It was 1959, six years after Stalin's death; Sputnik had been sent into space, the exhibit "America" opened up in the Soviet Union and the great spy thriller *North by Northwest* by Hitchcock was the rave of the day—in the Western Hemisphere, at least. Stalin's winter had been followed by the Khruschev Thaw, and Leningrad sleet. With a warmer official wind, cultural life in the country began to change long before any real political changes were possible. Clubs ranging from knitting to geology, from soccer to cinema sprang up inside official palaces of culture like mushrooms after rain. They had their own flags, badges, anthems and election ceremonies that gently mimicked the Soviet rituals. At the time KZBZ was the friendliest of the people's republics; with humor as the official ideology. On the day of my birth my father played it safe: betting on Zenit to lose, he won. In his jubilant mood he proposed that his first (and, as it would turn out, only) child be called Zenita, in honor of his favorite losing team. Besides, Zenita had a nice cosmic ring to it, referring to a point on the celestial sphere directly above the observer on Earth. My grandmothers were in uproar. While they rarely agreed between themselves, both liked the name Sasha, in which each letter evoked some dead or remote relative. It was common for Jewish families to give the children Russified versions of Jewish names; my father was Yuri rather than Uri and my mother acquired the poetic name Musa (the Muse) rather than be called Miriam. Like other Jewish families, mine lost many relatives through wars and Stalin's purges. To my knowledge, however, none was called Sasha; this name then became a generic collective commemoration. When my grandmothers uncovered my father's plot to call me Zenita, they became so horrified that they quickly agreed to the name Svetlana, my mother's favorite. In the Western imagination the name is linked to Stalin's daughter, but in the Soviet Union it has no association so specific. The name was actually popularized by the nineteenth-century Romantic Vassily Zhukovsky. In his ballad Svetlana appears as a curious blond girl who tries to read her future in a dim magic mirror. "I wish you never knew those morbid dreams, oh my Svetlana," the author cautioned his heroine. "Svetlana," means "sweetness and light," and in the 1970s the name also figured in a popular Soviet song about a first love that befalls a teenage boy in the middle of a tedious ninth-grade lesson on god knows what. You, the male lover, are swimming in a sea of boredom, left to your own devices in the pre-iPhone era, surfing the stormy seas of your unplugged adolescent imagination. " ... and there was spring waving at you from beyond the school window, a spring by the name of Svetlana."

Svetlana has many derivatives, Svetka, Svetik, Svetochka, all with a different suffix of endearment. I always felt like a girl of many names. In high school, I liked to have imaginary friends and identify with fictional characters. While I did not receive a proper Jewish education, which was strictly prohibited at the time, I was marked as "Jewish" in the ethnicity line of the school journal, which all school hooligans loved to explore. Eighty percent of the kids were registered as "Russian" and then there would be some oddballs: one Tatar, one Georgian, one Ukrainian, three Jews and a few "Russians" with suspicious foreign roots in their surnames, the crypto-Jews. I embraced my foreignness with a vengeance and loved to play spy games with my best friend, a Crimean Tatar by the name of Olya U. I used to love foreign fairy tales—from "The Little Mermaid," who emigrated from the beautiful underwater kingdom to the cruel earth, and "Little Red Riding Hood," who took a deviant path through the forest and cheated on the predator wolf with her brave undigested grandma. At the same time, I was taken with the Russian folk hero Ivan the Fool, who got an order to go "there, nobody knows where, to find that nobody knows what"—and he traveled to some fairy tale cosmos or near abroad.

Around age nine I wanted to become a Young Pioneer. I drew my inspiration from Bella Ilynichna, a half-blind veteran member of the Bolsheviks with whom my grandma had spent a few years in the camps of the Gulag in 1949–1954. Becoming a Young Pioneer was a striking experience of touch and smell. In a half-lit stadium called "The Jubilee" (where Zenit once played) we were lined up in our ironed white shirts and blue skirts, against the backdrop of velvety red banners with embroidered golden words. We were poised between childhood and something new, excited to touch our Pioneer kerchiefs and join the chorus of the future. Trembling with enthusiasm, I watched our chief Pioneer leader approach me from the end of the line. I was so eager to tie that knot of belonging. The next thing I sensed was the blast of the alcoholic breath of the chief Pioneer leader next to my excited face. His hands were shaking and he could barely make the kerchief's ends meet. And the knot came out loose. "Pioneers," screamed the prerecorded voice on the loud speaker. "For the struggle of the Communist Party, be ready!" "Always Ready!" the voice of the newly anointed Sveta Goldberg joined the chorus, only slightly off-key. I never liked the stories of young hero-pioneers, like Pavlik Morozov, the goody-goody boy who informed on his father, the supposed Kulak (a little more entrepreneurial peasant) under pressure from his loving mother but really for the sake of his Soviet Motherland. The little Soviet Oedipus wasn't my kind of hero. I didn't fall for the positive heroines either, blond and docile damsels who often got the guy. In my reading I moved a few centuries backwards and to foreign lands and empathized with the long-suffering and much misunderstood femme fatales who usually fared badly. My favorites were Milady de Winter in *The Three Musketeers*, she with the fleur-de-lis tattooed on her shoulder, and the dark and passionate Isadora Covarrubio de los Llanos, who snatched her enemies with a lasso in a forgotten American classic, *The Headless Horseman* by Captain Mayne Reid. There was also a red-haired Jewish adventuress, Rebecca in Walter Scott's *Ivanhoe*. Shoshana? I tried hard to salvage her from the status of a minor character. Literature was providing us a narrow escape from the Soviet everyday life that sometimes seemed to be an unreadable world of double speak and compromise in which there was so little correspondence between what was said and what was meant. Sharing books was an alternative form of belonging that involved not fitting in but being misfits together.

At thirteen I filled my address book with the improbable French-Russian name Mitya Brounié. We endured passionate caresses at the entrance to Gorky subway station and then on the roof of Peter and Paul Fortress. No, you wouldn't find "Mitya plus Sveta equals love" in yellow chalk there, we were too cool for that. Once I deliberately lost my address book and my secret lover became the subject of school gossip. After that Mitya never called back. None of my lovers to come, real or virtual, lived up to Mitya Brounié. Around age fifteen I fell in love with poetry as I smelled with veneration the thin dark blue volume of Osip Mandelshtam, published for the first time in 1972, after thirty-five years of silence. I don't know how my parents managed to afford this book. Its value on the black market at the time equaled the monthly salary of a Soviet engineer. My favorite poem "The Golden Stream of Honey," which I intuited rather than fully understood, unfolded in the Crimean town of Koktebel, where I spent my summer vacations. We enjoyed misty hills by the sea called "The Breasts of the Queen of Sheba" and gathered semi-precious stones with bifurcating veins like the lines of improbable fates. They were our ephemeral talismans that would connect the past and the future. Mandelshtam's poem flows slowly through the terraced landscapes of Koktebel like a golden-hued stream of honey in the dry Crimean heat. Mandelshtam believed that a poet or his ideal reader is a "poetic hermaphrodite," who moves freely between genders, ages and borders and communicates happily with his non-contemporaries across the world. Crimea embodied a "nostalgia for world culture," it was a unique part of Soviet territory where once upon a time Greeks, Italians, Scythians, Khazars, Jews, Tatars, Armenians and others intermingled and many cosmopolitan utopian visions flourished, including a bohemian paradise of artists and poets in the 1910s and a precarious dreamland called "Red Zion," a short-lived Jewish socialist dreamland in the 1920s.

In the poem "The Golden Stream of Honey" a beautiful red-haired hostess looks over her bared shoulder as her friends feast on conversation and flirtation on the verge of revolution and a bloody civil war, marking a perfect moment. At the end an uninvited guest appears. It is Odysseus. He comes home carrying tall tales, only his true home is not his native Ithaca but Crimea/Tauris, the land of exiles. "Odysseus returned filled with time and space." "Odysseus returned," echoes a poet from another continent and in another tongue. "But where is that man who said that Nobody was his name?" Jorge Luis Borges' *Ulysses* looks over his shoulder to catch his adventurous shadow.

The poetic Spanish of Jorge Luis Borges became my next language of choice. After high school I wanted to study foreign languages and cultures at Leningrad State University. However, my father learned through a friend in his film club, a professor at the university, that there were unofficial Jewish quotas and a girl with my last name "Goldberg" would never get in, however high her grades. My father didn't believe that anti-Semitism had survived Stalinism, but he didn't want to sacrifice my future to his high principles. He learned that the only place "accepting Jews" in the humanities that year was, for untold reasons of Soviet internal policies, the Spanish department of the Leningrad State Pedagogical Institute. The department was a true refuge for eccentrics. Our professors included a short and stocky linguistic wizard named Dr. Shabbes, an assistant professor from Baku, tall as Don Quixote, who played guitar and sang in the Basque language, a phonetics teacher named María-Luisa Muñoz, who was brought out of Spain as a child of nine during the Spanish Civil War and always dreamed of returning to her native Asturias, a handful of old Gulag survivors who had volunteered to fight in the Spanish Civil War at the age of eighteen and ended up imprisoned, and a few bland Soviet apparatchiks with good accents. Their role was to make sure the students didn't listen to the Beatles and kept their hair to the normative length. María-Luisa was responsible for my improbably pure Spanish accent, Castellano castizo, that continues to mislead people. For all our love for her, she used to torture us with phonetic exercises as if transmitting to us the physiognomy of her nostalgia. There was Don Quixote's monologue on freedom: "La li—ber—ta—d, Sancho, don't mumble, every sound loud and clear, let the very tip of your tongue kiss your front teeth silently … la libertad—it's not for the weak-hearted." The other required memorization was the Spanish poem about Little Red Riding Hood, caperu—ci—ta—en-carnada. "Caperu—c—ii—ta! Stretch your lips, girls like a sharp blade, until it hurts … don't mind the character lines! Ca-pe-ru—ciiiiii—ta." I heard that María-Luisa left for Madrid on the first available flight in the early days of perestroika.

The quixotic Spain that I discovered at Leningrad State Pedagogical Institute, an imaginary land of Soviet eccentric dreams, quickly became my patria chica. I became interested in the Iberian dialects and minority languages of Spain, such as Galician and Catalan or Ladino. Those poetic languages of the Middle Ages had much more in common among themselves than they did with the central Castilian that became the national language after the reunification of the country. I imagined my distant relative, the red-haired Spanish-Jewish girl Shoshana, escaping the moonlit roads of Toledo, crossdressing for the trip and writing poems to her maiden friends in different romance languages. "Muero porque no muero", I am dying because I am not dying. No, not like Santa Teresa la conversa, the great mystic. Mine would go like that: "Vivo, porque no vivo." (I live because I don't live.) "Porque la vida es sueño y los sueños sueños son" ("Because life is a dream and dreams are just dreams."—the last line is not Shoshana's). At the age of eighteen I spent my days in the library copying by hand the works on general and historic linguistics—from Saussure to Amado Alonso, deriving special pleasure from this narrow escape into scholarship.

My infatuation with Provencal and Catalan culminated with a romance with the professor-troubadour from Baku. Start small, he used to mentor me. Begin your research with a small specific thing, for example, the article in Catalan dialect. Then you can do something original and expand from there. Sorry, dear M.V., I was never able to follow your advice even though it came with lovely bouquets of roses, long walks through the Leningrad yards, husky Spanish love songs with a guitar accompaniment and a glass of Rkatsetelli, that young Georgian wine. Our romance ended up being mostly platonic, but it propelled me into emigration and a life of scholarship. I am still not good at staying with small things and can rarely distinguish the definite from the indefinite. But those suppressed romance languages lead me on a road of adventure and self-discovery.

Her life-changing chance encounter happened in 1979 in line for the sundried vobla in Koktebel, Crimea not far from the wine-dark sea. It couldn't have happened anywhere else. In that line she met a dashing Moscow architect with a golden-hued beard. His name sounded like a perfect artistic pseudonym, Constantin Boym. After a ten-minute conversation he asked her if she would like to go to America with him. The rest is history (and the subject of another story). Eventually she said yes, not there and then, but rather soon. They married in two months and began the process of relinquishing Soviet citizenship and obtaining an exit visa. They both kept their names—Boym and Goldberg and different artistic identities. The move from internal emigration into an external one seemed like a continuity, but actually this was more of a leap of faith. Internal émigré is someone who distances, estranges herself as far as politically possible from the engagements and compromises of her society and carves a state within a state for herself, sometimes as small as a "kitchen salon." There she shares her immigrant identity at her own risk with likeminded people. The borders of these states within states are unguarded and porous, but still the internal émigré follows (and deviates) from the mother-tongue and the home country. When you emigrate abroad, especially from a closed and closely-knit society, you experience a shock from the very idea that there is an "abroad" there. In our case, it was hard to believe that the "West" was not merely an ideological or countercultural fiction; it operates according to the rules of a different language altogether. We knew well our point of departure but not our destination. The "West" existed for us as the other and as a movie land. Our actual experiences didn't always follow the movie scripts. It was daring Svetka, repulsed by injustice and enamored of other lives, who decided to emigrate from the Soviet Union promptly and decisively.

The process was humiliating and unpleasant. The crypto-Jewish professor in the Spanish department (Professor Shabbes? Is this possible that such was his name?) asked me to voluntarily withdraw from the Pedagogical Institute risking never to finish my education in the Soviet Union. Alternatively, the administration would have to conduct a long public meeting shaming me as a traitor of the motherland, which would be unpleasant for everyone. I chose to drop out "for family reasons." Two years after my emigration, my father was made the target of a mini show trial at his factory; he was accused of rearing a traitor of the motherland. He was fired from his job and removed from his post as president of his film club "Kino and You." The only job he could find was as a night guard in a parking lot, where he read a lot of foreign detective stories and began to learn English. After being thrown out of the Pedagogical

Institute and subsequently applying to emigrate, I spent a year and a half in Soviet limbo, not quite an émigré, not quite a refusenik. Times were tense. The Moscow Olympic Games brought smiley Olympic bears and less smiley beefy policemen all over the place. I finally received an exit visa to leave for "permanent residence" in the state of Israel. Several months of transit camps in Austria and Italy followed, and at the end, I chose to come to the United States, ending up in Boston, which I thought was Leningrad's American sister city. At the interview with the immigration agency, an officer kept my husband's name Constantin Boym intact, but suggested I change mine: "Nobody in America would be able to pronounce your first name Svetlana. How about Susan?" The woman asked cheerfully. "It's easy enough to pronounce." I opted for Suzanne because I used to love the song "Suzanne, believe me, I am sorry, Suzanne forever..." (There must have been a good reason for him to be making excuses, and I hope Suzanne didn't believe him.) The immigration officer smiled at me and scribbled something on my non-resident alien application form. "Sveta Goldberg" walked out "Susan Boym." I wasn't upset about the name change.

I didn't feel robbed of my identity. I felt liberated and hoped to reinvent myself. There was a small glitch with Susan. A new acquaintance would call on the phone and ask: "Can I speak to Sue?" "You've got the wrong number," I would answer politely. I liked my new American name, but I never learned to respond to it. Susan was one of my most assimilated American selves. During the first year in America, Susan had a brief career as a part-time secretary at a place called Matching Roommates. She went to Filene's Basement and purchased a pink-and-white checkered shirt with a white collar to look like a secretary in a commercial for something like yogurt. Not too long ago, I found myself at Downtown Crossing in Boston, where I did my first American shopping. Where Filene's Basement used to be, there was a gaping hole in the ground in the heart of Boston, on the border between the historic center and the business district, an unfinished communal grave of the immigrant bargain hunting experience. The Matching Roommates office was located in a leaking basement in Brighton and while I passed for a diligent new American at the job interview, I was promptly fired after failing to buy my boss the right smoked turkey and Dijon mustard sandwich. All I remember from that experience was the boss's thick moustache, like in a Mayakovsky poem I learned in high school, "Hey, you, mistah, you've got cabbage in your moustache," and a rotten bench in the high grass in Fenway Park. Whenever he would send me out of the basement into some special reconnaissance mission, I would take my break on that bench and read my yard-sale copy of *The Love Story*, blissfully forgetting what kind of dressing my boss was after. As a former communal apartment dweller, I was suspicious of matching roommates and of Dijon mustard. My next American job was a real labor of love. I became a part-time aide to the social worker in the Jewish Family and Children Service (JFS), assigned to work with Cuban refugees. I had to accompany them from their shelter in Dorchester to the JFS and to the welfare office to help them with their asylum seeking, benefits and employment. My group consisted of three Cuban men, two tall brothers who were still in a state of shock or stupefaction from their departure and smoked quite a lot of dope, which made it challenging to wake them up and persuade them to come to their appointments—all of that using my nineteenth-century Soviet Castilian. The third man was short and soulful. He told me in confidence that he was a skilled mechanic and was determined "to make it in America." I can still hear the faltering steps of the three men behind my back as if I were their Pioneer leader. They called me Susana and also respectfully Nue-tra Mae-tra. We often had to understand each other with half-words. Of course, I never told on them even when the kind social worker asked me point blank if they were clean. One thing I learned in the Soviet Union, never to be a snitch. I just wanted them to wake up and not jeopardize their support. Once in the Welfare Office in the city, a famous monument of Brutalist Architecture, I would have to accompany them and do a trickster translation, inventing and embellishing their stories of years of work experience back in Cuba. Gringa as I was, we were still compañeros de la lucha. Then they were transferred somewhere else. On our last meeting they gave me three glass heart pins—green, red and blue. Por Nue-tra Mae-tra. The safety pins broke but the glass hearts are still with me, somewhere in my unsorted archive. Years passed and I became a resident alien and a proud green-card carrier (exposing my left ear in the identity photograph) and finally, a citizen. In my heart I remain a resident alien, even though now I co-own an attached single house and no longer own up to my former immigrant resilience. I know, I know. A resident alien is better as a poetic metaphor than a living condition. Going to graduate school in literature was like coming home. It offered me an alternative to conventional immigrant assimilation and a true home—a portable one—in world literature. When I was asked at the Jewish Vocational Services, which was helping to resettle Soviet refugees, what job preparation I was looking for, I said that I wanted to go back to university. After all, that's one of the reasons I left and I only finished three years of education. What field? the officer asked. Philosophy, I said, or philology.

That sounded like a joke to the immigration office. A practical vocation, indeed. He said that the best he could do was a three-month intensive typing course, possibly with programming thrown in. I slammed the door in response. Then I took the subway to the Boston Public Library and spent an afternoon researching universities in Boston. I inquired about "minority grants" for Jewish women and it was politely explained to me that Jews in America no longer needed support in getting a university education. I also learned that there was such a thing as a "deadline" and it passed. Not too alarmed by the information that I had obtained officially, I decided to simply go to the departments and knock on some doors. Boston University was the closest. Trembling a little, I walked to the office of the chair of the Modern Languages Department. Through the half-cracked door, I was surprised to see a youngish man sitting with his feet up on the desk reading a book about Bertolucci. Even though he was quite puzzled by my refugee traveling documents and my transcripts from the Pedagogical Institute that listed many courses in "military services" and "civil defense nursing practice," he proved to be open-minded. We hit it off speaking about the one topic I knew something about—Italian communist cinema. In 1981, Spanish-speaking Soviet refugees were still an exotic commodity and without my knowing it I dressed the part, in my beige coat and long straight hair. He suggested that I speak with the Spanish professor next door, Alicia B. I couldn't believe the openness and access that I was able to gain without any letter, connection, favor, barter, or what in Russian was called "blat"—a combination of all of the above.

Alicia proved to be even more fascinating, a beautiful and mysterious writer and scholar, and herself a Polish Jewish refugee from Argentina. I was a little surprised that she spoke to me in some version of sixteenth-century Spanish "vos sabes" but I didn't show it and tried my best. She was equally surprised by my "overall good" grades in military nursing but chose to overlook it. She asked me if I could just come the next day and teach a class in elementary Spanish. I had enough chutzpa to say yes. The class went fine, language teaching skills proved to be transferrable. The only thing I didn't understand was when the students made conversation about some mysterious "General Hospital," since the words "soap opera" were not yet in my vocabulary. I also didn't know that there are letter grades and not the usual 5, 4, 3, 2, 1. Later at the orientation meeting at Boston University, an Italian professor, a one-year veteran of the American education system, taught me an important life lesson: "In an American university, you're better off not asking questions. Otherwise you can reveal how much you don't know."

Alicia's husband, a major scholar of French literature named Jeffrey Mehlman, happened to be the head of the Master's Program. They came up with a low-risk Solomonian solution. I will teach elementary Spanish, which my education in pedagogy qualified me to do, with a good Asturian accent, and I would be able to take classes in the MA program part-time for free. This was when I thought that I had really made it. I found my true homeland— the Fourth International of American Immigrants. Today the story seems unbelievable to me; it would probably not happen today, in the highly bureaucratic university environment. In other words, as I sit on the admission committees with my distinguished colleagues, I realize over and over again that today I probably wouldn't make it into the graduate school of a major university. Now that I serve on many committees, I try to be a "fifth column," so to speak, to sneak in an unusual and eccentric person, an immigrant or not, flawed but original. (shsh …)

So, once I started to build a second home in America as a part-time teacher of Spanish, I decided to travel abroad—to Spain, of course, to study Catalan at a special program in the monastery in Palma de Mallorca. Susana, the student of oppressed Iberian dialects, was getting back on the road. The program included a roundtrip fare on Spantax and I proudly showed my new "Refugee Travel Document" on the US border. At that time, I was still a "non-resident alien." However, upon my landing in Spain, I was immediately arrested at Barajas Airport and was threatened with deportation. My "Refugee Travel Document" (with the line in capital letters on the first page "This Is Not a Passport of the United States of America" seemed suspicious. The concept of a Soviet Jew immigrating to America to study Catalan didn't seem too plausible. Deportation and loss of scholarship didn't sound appealing, so I went for the arrest. One glitch was that the airline had allowed me to board the plane, so they were supposed to guarantee my entry into the country. For the night I was placed in an extraterritorial glass room, sleeping on uncomfortable chairs, but during the day I was allowed into the lobby, where vendors kindly offered me churros con chocolate for free as a sweet neighborly gesture. Once again, my Castilian accent helped a lot, as did a slim volume of Jorge Luis Borges' *Fictions*, which was traveling with me. I lay on three loosely assembled chairs in my Barajas revolutionary cell, leaving greasy chocolate stains on the fictional pages of the encyclopedia of Tlon. Ulysses in a skirt came home to her patria chica, but she was mistaken for that woman whose name was Nobody. There was no Cyclope, only the buff airport police officer. For four or five days, literature helped me survive and I was imagining what this airport limbo would look like from the perspective of Tlon. Finally, I came up with a more practical solution and found my Spanish professor from Boston University, who happened to be teaching summer school in Madrid. He kindly agreed to appear on my behalf at the police station and offer something called "A moral evaluation of S's character and behavior." This sounded very Soviet. I still don't know what else he did for me, but finally I was lectured briefly on how to be a "law abiding" and moral citizen and traveler, and my "Refugee Travel Document" was properly stamped and I was allowed to step on Spanish soil.

Madrid in 1982 had nothing of the colorful spirit of Almodovar that we have come to associate with the urban boom of the 1990s. Only six years after Franco's death, the Spanish capital struck me as a beautiful but grim Eastern European place with shady stocky men whispering obscenities in a good Castilian accent as I walked around Plaza del Sol. I inhabited the narrow space of a Madrileño balcony, which keeps you on your toes and forever on the threshold, stuck in the window frame in front of the cast iron Saturn. On the whole my Spanish homecoming was not a success. In the school for the study of Catalan, I stood out as an odd bird, a Russian-American who could barely afford a meal out. While my Spanish professors back in Leningrad dreamed of returning to Spain, the locals wanted to go back to the USSR of the Spanish Republican imagination of their parents, quite an understandable nostalgia after Franco's repression of memory, but strange for me at the time. America, on the other hand, was considered Reagan's evil empire and nobody could figure out why I would have left the USSR for the USA. But when curiosity subsided, the students who came from different Catalan-speaking provinces of the country mostly argued among themselves about true and impostor Catalan. Which was the most primordial and authentic? Which would unite the Catalan lands: Barcelones? Valencia? Menorqui? Mallorchi? I was also embarrassed about my financial restrictions that kept me out of many outdoor cafes. Mostly, I spent my time in the monastery garden reading the great

Catalan philosopher Raimon Llull and Jorge Luis Borges, in the politically incorrect language of power—Castilian Spanish.

Before my departure for the US, I had an uncanny encounter in a Madrid park where I was having my beloved churros con chocolate that smudged the pages of Borges' *Fictions*. A young man with an unruly beard approached me and then started talking in a strangely accented Spanish. "Why don't you speak to me in your native language? He whispered." Pause. "Are you afraid? Why are you hiding something?" He made me nervous. "Yo soy Gallego, tu eres Gallega … let's talk to each other right." (I am Galician, you're Galician.) Unbelievable. This man mistook me for a native! He was no KGB agent with a fake beard following Svetlana Goldberg on a trip abroad. No. I, Susana, with my heavy Russian-Asturian "ese-s" was taken to be a Spaniard from the next province to the West. How many times I dreamed of being Spanish during my language classes in Leningrad and Boston? I had finally passed successfully. But at that moment I chose not to prolong this imaginary communion. "I am American, not Galician." I said, surprising myself. This was the first time I dared to say it: I am American. I already knew it would have been much better to say "I am Russian." A pause of incomprehension. "I am American," I repeated. "Soy Americana." Pause. Another pause. Hiss. "Hueles a Yanqui!" (You smell like a Yankee.) (I hasten to add that I fell in love with Spain, belatedly, in 2009. I traveled all over Catalunya with great pleasure. I took part in an exhibit "Historiar-Imaginar" devoted to Spanish recovery of memory of Franco, suppressed during the roaring 90s and thought that somehow this country's forgetting mirrored mine. My new affection is a lasting and mature affection that almost wiped out the failures of this gritty romance.)

Not the specific country, Spain, but literature itself proved to be the best immigrant homeland, the new immigrant international. Maybe I never learned how to drive a car but I had plenty in my imagination and a poetic driving license. In the 1980s the American university turned out to be a reliable refuge for immigrants; it gave us scholarships and a sense of adventurous belonging. During my first, most bookish years in America I felt that I was really living. "Life and death I've long put in quotes like fabulations known to be empty," wrote the Russian poet Marina Tsvetaeva. In my research that would become my first book, I explored different personae, masks and deep selves, and the myths of the poet in life and death. "Life and Death in Quotation Marks," was to be my first book title. The editor at Harvard University Press thought that it was too long and suggested cutting either life or death. At the age of twenty-eight *Death in Quotation Marks* seemed to me a sexier title, although what drove me really was life—expanding life in and out of literature into the world.

While believing in the power of ideas, I was always cautious about translating texts back into life or making any kind of ready-made models of transcendence. The poet's stories were exemplary experiments and transformation of the self that moved in and out of the dangerous border zone of life and death. In my twenties, I was traveling the world recklessly like Dona Quixote trying to live out the lessons of literature. I followed the surrealist guide to Paris and read Georges Bataille's *Interior Experience* and André Breton's *Nadja* over a single short cup of coffee in the café Bonaparte—one per day was as much as I could afford. I was waiting for the mind-blowing existential chance encounter while the local Parisians were just minding their own everyday business over overflowing café au lait and decadent deserts. The only "chance encounter" I had was with a Hungarian immigrant who read the same books but was even poorer than I. Our romance culminated with him asking me to buy him a sandwich. Yet I wasn't too disappointed. Life was a romance—not in the sense of a love affair but in the sense of a quest. My first youth in the Soviet Union was cut short by the difficult process of emigration. I was hoping to catch up during my second American youth. At the age of twenty I married the adventurous architect I met in the line for beer and vobla, but rather than a conventional marriage, Constantin and me created a unique partnership for exploring the world and ourselves. We were bent on discovering something new every year. We didn't want to assimilate into American middle-class life. The "American dream" of a little suburban house was foreign to us.

I remember reading Marx in my high school, my girlfriend Kycha and I found two "classes" that were considered particularly hideous and despised in Marxist–Leninist edifice; the "social strata intelligentsia" (to which the leaders themselves belonged) and the "lumpen-proletariat" that anarchically challenged the heroic working class. I was clearly low-class "intelligentsia" according to the Soviet class system but aspired to be a lumpen-aristocrat, a Leningrad girl-dandy. In America I wanted to be a hard-working and not heavily drinking bohemian who can avoid suffering from hunger, tuberculosis or epilepsy like the characters of nineteenth-century novels. I learned later that many of the surviving American bohemians that I met in the mid-1980s were trust fund kids. I loved Nabokov's confession about the pleasure of exile: "The break in my own destiny allowed me a syncopal kick that I wouldn't have changed for worlds." Syncope means at once a missed beat in a musical composition, a shortage of breath and a swoon; it brought together the loss of bodily control and the intricate composition. Syncopal composition was about a piercing experience of sensual details without synthesis, a vertiginous suspension in the air. I seemed to have sailed into immigration gingerly, like Ivan the Fool on a magic carpet; fairy tales were almost coming true if only I could keep memories and gaps in my story at bay. Unlike Lot's wife I didn't care to look back. There was still so much I had to look forward to. In other words, it was all going as planned, until one day, some six years into my American life, I started to have dreams of Russia.

They came slowly but steadily, at a time when I barely spoke Russian with anyone. I rushed through the same transit space, a long corridor of an anonymous communal apartment turning into a half-lit railway station; always a passage from one nowhere to another, crowded third-class train cars with people's legs hanging from the upper bunks, loose locks on the doors of strangely shaped rooms in communal apartments filled with friends and relatives whose faces I barely recognized. They always waited for me, yet I caught them unawares. I would try to escape and there would always be another room there and then another. I still follow these passages in my dreams and no number of trips to Russia has cured me of them. Then came a very stark and simple dream. I found myself in the middle of St. Isaac Square (the dark statue in the center, purple pomposity of the huge cathedral, drizzle in the air, sleet on the uneven boardwalks). I need to go to Senate Square to the monument of the Bronze Horseman (grey waves frozen in stones, mad hooves and the undulating serpent underneath, the Tsar's unseeing eyes). Somehow, I cannot get there. I walk in circles and there is no way to get there. Well, every Leningradian knows that the squares are adjacent; one behind the other on a straight line. In the dream the straight line turned into an endless spiral. When I woke up, I would start drawing maps of Leningrad public transportation, trolleys and buses going from my house to different parts of the city. Here was Trolley No 1 moving along the wide avenues to the imperial glory of palaces and bridges over the rippling river. Tram No 6 crawled through the click and clacker of the dark outskirts, the dirty Karpovka River and Spanish-language high school near the Botanic garden where I practiced my "pedagogy." And there was the crowded Bus No 49 going to St. Isaac Square; the driver on this bus deeply hated his passengers and loved leaving them behind, cutting short their hopes to make it on time.

I started writing my memoir of public transportation in a pre-computer age and it might still be somewhere in my papers or lost during one of my American relocations. And then the eighties came to a dramatic end; the Berlin Wall was suddenly cracking and falling—with its bright pop art on one side and grim concrete on the other. I wanted to touch the burning stones of history on the streets of Berlin and Leningrad, which seemed much more relevant than all my academic quotation marks. The fracture in my personal destiny corresponded to the breaks in collective history, where forgetting was also a central feature, much less discussed than the restoration of collective memory. In 1989 the iron curtain was dismantled and many rejoiced in their personal colorful pieces of the Berlin Wall. The Soviet Union ceased to exist in 1991 and the whole country felt like the country of immigrants, even though many didn't move very far. I remember the Moscow Summer of August 1991 was a euphoric time in Russian history when thousands of people came to express support for perestroika and glasnost against the attempted Putsch. Moreover, similar to the Velvet revolution in Prague, this was a voluntary civic protest (without Twitter and Facebook aid) that hadn't happened in Russia since the February revolution. While this major historical event—much maligned and deliberately misinterpreted later—was taking place, no TV channel was willing to show it. Instead all TV channels were showing *Swan Lake*, the great Tchaikovsky's ballet, morning, day and night. That was how everyone knew that something was terribly wrong and couldn't be reported. I had just returned to the US a couple of weeks before and was in constant contact with my friends from the Leningrad TV program *The Fifth Wheel* who were reporting from the Palace Square where they were facing old Soviet tanks. "Call CNN," the anchorman was insisting. I couldn't disappoint him by saying that I had no direct line to the recently created CNN. On CNN, the advance of tanks on Red Square in Moscow and the Palace Square in Leningrad as well as the euphoric and brave reactions of the protesters were constantly interrupted by the advance of the mysterious "Hurricane Bob" on Boston and the warnings about candles, pipes and floods. Since my Soviet years, I believed that whenever people speak excessively about the weather, there might be something else going on that they are covering up. "Small talk" must be concealing something big that cannot be talked about. All those babbling brooks and forest lakes usually appeared on Soviet TV channels as lovely nature intermissions to avoid controversial reporting. Of course, when it came to the revolution, like August 1991, it was time for something more unnatural, like *Swan Lake* as a little less natural.

Following CNN on August 20, my friend from the St. Petersburg TV station was screaming into my phone receiver. "Sveta, what the hell is going on? What disaster? Who is Bob? CIA?" At that historic moment I lost power and remained in absolute darkness in my house in Boston with no candles and no saved water. I realized that not all weather reports are ideological, and that I am doomed to miss history. After this August putsch of 1991, the media opened up and till the Putin era it was multifaceted, experimental and diverse. But that *Swan Lake* moment will come back with a vengeance in the 2000s. Many people welcomed the change after the wall came down in 1989 and the Soviet Union ended in 1991. Like true émigrés who knew what they left behind but not where they were going. Yet a large number of former Soviet citizens didn't feel that such emigration was their choice; in Russian culture we often had quicker access to blame than to reflection and responsibility. Eventually the difficulties and perceived economic injustices of the transition, as well as enforced forgetting of life experiences during the Soviet era, opened the road of restorative nostalgia for the world that might have existed in their dreams, and in their dreams only.

I took my first trip back to Russia in 1990 after nine years abroad. For at least six of those years I hadn't imagined such a return trip was possible. I was told on the Soviet border in 1981 that I would never be allowed back to see my parents, and I was stripped of my Soviet citizenship. In 1990 as the British aircraft started to circle down to earth and I could see the shabby building of the Leningrad airport, I became paralyzed and didn't wish to leave the international territory. But I was accompanying a sixteen-year-old distant cousin who was going for the first time to see her father in Russia, so I had to get up and dare, for her. For ten years I went back several times a year and every time I dreaded the arrival and mourned the departure from Russia and all the deep friendships I built there. But once on the plane out, I would always be possessed by the vertiginous happiness of an immigrant—wow, I managed to leave again! I began my book *The Future of Nostalgia* with an anti-nostalgic premise. Immigrants of the first generation often had a taboo on nostalgia. Moreover, this particular longing for home was most used and abused by nationalist politicians and religious extremists—a longing for a grander patria that existed in some historic moment that is now turned into an eternal present. I defined nostalgia as a longing for home that no longer exists or perhaps had never existed. Most importantly, nostalgia seems to be a longing for a place but in fact it's a yearning for another time; it can be also a rebellion against the irreversibility of modern time, a desire for slower rhythms of existence. Nostalgia has a utopian element to it, only the utopia is not directed toward the future but towards the past or towards "another time" more broadly. The more I worked on nostalgia, the more I realized that it might be incurable and its object is forever elusive. It is better to face up to one's nostalgias for all that matters is that we don't fall into a collective manipulation of our affects and make our own serpentine road of longing. I distinguished between "restorative nostalgia" that is anti-historical and tries to restore the space of the great homeland often engaging conspiracy theories and myths and "reflective nostalgia" that knows that is has no single object and explores affectionately the human experience of time. Nostalgia is not always retrospective; it can also be prospective, it can move sideways and open the roads not taken, a past future that never came to be. I became very attuned to the seductions and discontents of this strange modern emotion that is best practiced in art and not in politics. And of course, nostalgia is not what it used to be. "Do you miss Russia?" I would be asked. "Yes, but it's not what you mean." Or I would say "No, but it's not what you think." What it was that I thought and felt remained off-limits to me. I felt a certain incongruity, like the closer I was to my home the stranger it looked. Homesickness would be followed by a sickness of home. It was not really a homecoming that was important for me but a desire to be a public intellectual who lives in history, shares cross-cultural experiences and can become an acute observer and possibly, an adviser who brings back knowledge to one's first motherland. Sometime in 1994, fifteen years since my study at the

Pedagogical Institute, I decided to visit my alma mater. I went spontaneously and anonymously, with my American boyfriend, not notifying anyone. The entrance with the shabby cracked paint looked exactly the same. In the buffet in the dark lobby the same lady "bufetchitsa" was selling cabbage pirozhki (I am tempted to say the same pirozhki for they looked pretty antique). In the girls' toilet which was our unofficial salon, there was a familiar smell of young sweat from a pre-deodorant era and there were a few freshmen with excited blushing faces and smudged blue shades who were discussing exams. It was very familiar but I never felt more out of place. I was almost afraid to speak English to my boyfriend, not to be arrested for illegitimate contact with foreigners. We went up to the third floor where the Spanish department used to be located. Since we spoke English, a few secretaries looked at us suspiciously through the cracks of the doors. The corridors were dark and empty; it must have been an intersession and a reading period for the exam. My boyfriend found the situation amusing; he started to explore the "Wall Papers" (nastenny gazety?) which portrayed students' achievement and progress—mostly in black and white, as if color photography hadn't reached the Pedagogical Institute yet.

"Here you are, he said suddenly. "What do you mean?" "That's you," he repeated. I looked at one of the photographs of the students' research and saw a girl with long straight hair with a familiar white pin, dark Polish jeans, a serious look. Behind her on the board were Spanish and Catalan verbs of motion, circa 1978. What happened to that girl, one might wonder? Maybe she became a researcher in this Institute? Unfortunately, her name was Goldberg so she went to teach in the English school on the outskirts somewhere. How was it possible that the persona non-grata and "traitor of the motherland" who was asked to quit the Institute in 1979 and asked never to come back was still hanging on the board of scientific research? My professor could have paid with a strict reprimand or demotion by the security department of the university. Did M.Z. the professor of Spanish and Basque keep it there nostalgically till the rainy day? Was it simply an act of Soviet negligence? Did they try to avoid the "brain drain" and keep Svetlana Goldberg in her alma mater? Was there no new research on Spanish verbs on motion since 1978? Somehow Svetlana Goldberg was detained on the board of scientific research in 1978 and lived on in this badly lit corridor in Leningrad–Petersburg for the last fifteen years, while Svetlana Boym went to another university, became a professor and escaped. Or at least, she thought she did. In the 1990s I hoped to be Russian-American and serve both cultures. Of course, I couldn't quite pass for a native in either of the two countries, in spite of my flawless Russian. It was the body language and the inappropriate smile that betrayed me on the streets of St. Petersburg and Moscow. And one more thing: whenever I tripped walking on the streets of my hometown, I would say 'shit, or "ouch"—always in English, betraying myself. After 1996 I could sense the change in the Russian zeitgeist looking at cultural projects, new architecture and urban transformations such as the building of the uncanny replica of the Cathedral of Christ the Saviour and of the largest shopping mall in Russia with Crimean motives in the center of Moscow. Crimea is Ours! Crimea is Russian! was an agenda of the Mayor of Moscow, Luzhkov, but it wasn't taken so seriously then and nobody objected to a few buildings that were not far from Red Square that were prefiguring what was to come nor the books that were sold en masse. In the summer of 1999 so many possibilities appeared still open, we had conversations about freedom in smokey cafes, meeting with potential liberal candidates to the post of prime minister. It all came to an end in early 2000. I abandoned the idea of being a dual citizen, de facto, if not de jure. In 2003 a policeman stopped me in central Moscow. "What is your nationality?" He asked. "What?" I was perplexed. "Nationality," he said rudely, "your documents." "I am a Jew," I said, "American by passport." "Oh, ok," he answered. "Don't worry. I thought you were a Caucasian" (in the Russian context someone from the Caucasus. In slang they are also called "darkies"). That was the time when one type of ethnic discrimination was temporarily superseded by another; I was still non-white in his eyes, only a less dangerous non-white. That's when the realization came that Sveta, who speaks Russian without an accent, is just as a much an imaginary creature as Susana, la Gallega, or Susan, the American

Russia does not tolerate hyphenated identities; you can never be Russian/and/and. Russian and Jewish and American and Catalan, for example. It's always either/or, more than in many other places in the world. Working with Russian culture you are frequently placed into a category of patriot or traitor, and rarely a translator. September 2001 reoriented many peoples' lives and turned them inward. For me with Vladimir Putin in Russia and George W. Bush in the United States, the decade of 2000 was the time of forgetting—and writing a book about alternative conceptions of public freedom that were vanishing all over the world. Freedom is a "new beginning and a miracle of infinite improbability," these words of Hannah Arendt opened up the world of inspiration. In the book I asked the question of how to live with uncertainty, how to co-create in the public space and make a new beginning possible without abandoning historical and personal memory. In the Russian conception there was always an opposition between inner freedom or "freer freedom" of will in which Russians excel and lack of political freedoms—from the time of the absolute monarchy to Stalinism. In Russian culture it's often more important to feel free at the moment than to learn how to live in freedom. Radical and mostly short-lived liberation is valued higher than a deliberate struggle for freedoms and laws. In fact, the positive concept of freedom (rather than liberation or independence) originated in the Athenian republic; it referred to public, not personal freedom and was particularly cherished by the former slaves and immigrants who had a chance to become citizens of Athens. In some ways, it was up to outsiders to appreciate and admire the possibility to live free that the natives might have taken for granted. As for the conceptions of inner freedom, these date back to the later Imperial time and internalized the public architecture. Stoics speak about the "acropolis of the soul" when the other Acropolis is in ruins. The public space of freedom was a space of co-creation, a performance with social conventions, laws and institutions but not limited to a technocratic practice and opening space for individual spontaneity and dissent. On the whole I tried to reinvent the humanistic and political conception of public freedom, something East European dissidents and other post-totalitarian thinkers dreamed about and valued higher than capitalist economy.

Working on a book on freedom was more of a solitary exercise than working on nostalgia. I found that my readers were more interested in the utopian attachment to the past than in uncertainty in the present and the future. After my own confrontation with uncertainty, I married my long-time American boyfriend. My nom de plume—Svetlana Boym, however, was left intact. During that time of Putin's power, I stopped traveling to Russia. In my Boston I found myself caught in an unintentional art project. I was cutting the photographs from my journeys to Russia and Eastern Europe in the 1990s, sometimes unique snapshots, with no backup. Then I began to arrange them into collages disfiguring images of home and leaving errors, overexposures and blurs. I preferred the fun of cutting and moving fragments over the old wallpaper to the fixity of pasting. But at the end the all-purpose glue and conventional framing made those ephemeral projects into "art." Then I began to work with minimal units of movement. My media projects "Phantasmagorias of History" and "Multitasking with Clouds" exposed historic images to chance and human error and revealed their cracks and the patina of time. I used the syncopated movement to assemble the images together, winking to Nabokov and his celebration of the missed beats. It was the "zero" decade of the twenty-first century and for better or for worse, "the end of history" was nowhere in sight. My disorganized archive was dispersed all over the house and I shrugged at the suggestion to write an immigrant memoir. In fact, I dreaded what seemed to be my own nostalgic turn. I sought forgetting for the sake of the new beginning. So, I found the website Improbable Reality, and it seemed to be a perfect new platform for intellectual experiments. The idea of posting your real name (or real face!) was alien to the free spirit of those early days. Improbable Reality required an interesting alias and a high-level of conversation. It focused on the philosophical quest and held forums on the nature of the real, on freedom and memory. I thought of using Zenita as my alias, Zenita, a wild digital pioneer without a red tie, but settled for Svoboda—freedom in Russian. Nobody got it; they assumed I was a man, called me informally, "Svobo" (and I hope nobody confused me with Slobodan). The Improbable Reality soon took over the probable one and I found myself writing to other philosophically minded aliases instead of answering my own emails. We had broad discussions about law and freedom; pleasure and memory. One feature was a continuous debate between a law professor with a pompous alias and two female academics. One presented an analytic feminist position while the other was a bit long-winded and idealistic. The professor usually got to do the punchline and the last word and somehow the others accepted this kindly. And then one day Improbable Reality suffered an identity crisis. As the homepage was migrating to another server, the organizers needed to verify information about the participants. At that time, they discovered that the "law professor" who argued with two feminist academics was pulling everybody's virtual leg. Actually, he impersonated all three characters, making two presumably female scholars a little less intelligent than himself. The founder of the Improbable Reality, a philosophy student from Amsterdam, had a Code of Honor. Each participant could select a fictional avatar—but then they had to enter into a real meaningful dialogue with OTHERS, not just with themselves. It was a good old-fashioned virtual salon where we abandoned our everyday identity for an intense international conversation on important subjects. You can go outside your everyday self but you still have to listen to others. I briefly exchanged emails with the founder and I think Zenita-Svoboda was the only woman on the site. Then the homepage migrated to a new platform that involved a more secure password which I eventually forgot.

Thus, the Improbable Reality collapsed as had my other ephemeral homelands. My first secret digital romance was, of course, in Spanish, in its unfamiliar poetic dialect of Spanish with many a hiatus and crafted silences. It crossed many borders and pushed the boundaries of the text and the body. It began with explicit courtship. My anonymous correspondent X had an intimate knowledge of *The Future of Nostalgia* as if he was the book's true addressee. X claimed that we never met outside the text and proceeded with an old-fashioned courtship mixing the quotes from Don Quixote and the Argentinian poet of Slavic descent Alejandra Pizarnik. We spoke about our exiles, young pioneers—in cold and hot climates, poems and syncopes. Who wouldn't fall for that? This was an old-fashioned epistolary romance, not virtual dating. We invented our own singular platform and a private language; only my correspondent didn't want to bring it into the non-virtual space. X was sometimes omnipresent and other times endlessly elusive. As we went deeper and deeper into language, writing more often, barely touching the tender buttons of the keyboard, just reading each other's immigrant minds, I began to realize that my Spanish did not have enough nuance of affect and irony. My Leningrad phonetic training was useless but I didn't admit to my linguistic limitations. In one particularly intricate letter I was caught in a web of allusions and suddenly faced a line that made no sense from the point of view of Spanish grammar: "Y que vas a decir si fuera una ella?" I chose to ignore this agrammatical line. (Try google translation, dear reader.) My correspondent was startled by my silence. Please answer. Is this so horrible? What if I were a she? So my caballero andante was also la belle dame sans merci, polymorphous and versatile. Somebody to whom the eros of language came naturally. I was Ezbed-lana for her, this was my name that was fully hers; it was saved for this singular romance between two immigrants from different continents. No, I wasn't writing to myself; for once I had a real addressee. These days, as I board a crowded subway car, I hear my name called: Sveta, Susana, Svetka, Svetlana. I turn around as if in a time machine and recognize nobody. I came to know too many people in different disjointed universes, so I don't connect names and faces any more, they float weightlessly in space like folded paper snowflakes from Soviet New Year parties. These names lived with me like the characters of unfinished novels, barely sketched and abandoned before reaching their full potential. I tried to pass for a native in too many countries—Russia, USA, Spain, Russia again, USA again. Now it is time to embrace my embarrassing accented self. But when will emigration finally end? It dawned on me only recently that it wasn't a one-time border crossing, but a life-long journey beyond my control. It is as if there is a strange engine inside me that makes me go in zigzags, like the knight in the game of chess. Victor Shklovsky wrote in the 1920s that he and his friends were still playing a game with certain rules, a chess game, but the world around them was engaged in a more cruel theater of trial, error and arbitrariness. The immigrant is a creature of contradictions: tough and vulnerable, excessively earnest and a compulsive masquerader, skeptical on the outside, trusting on the inside. Never uttering a casual "I love you" but always dreaming of being able to say it and mean it, at times a clairvoyant and at other times, willfully blind, caught up in aspirations for the future and fears of the unburied past in a country that no longer exists.

After some improbable things come true in your life, as they did in mine, you start to rely on the exceptional and trust your luck. Not a good idea. The immigrant is a trickster who can easily be tricked at her own game. She is susceptible to pyramid schemes of happiness and gets swindled over and over again, whether the scheme be the perfect middle-class nest that she occasionally envies, with cuddly spooning in bed, with less writing and more living, or a perfect intellectual community somewhere in a good climate, a non-Platonic Symposium for women. The immigrant is easy prey both for improbable adventure and for the promise of security and comfort. She is an unstoppable gambler who suddenly realizes that she no longer knows the rules of the game. It's tempting to turn exile into a metaphor; exile from paradise, exile into humanity, exile into art. If you came to

America as a child of immigrants and went to an American school and later to a creative writing program, you know the exact genre for speaking about immigrant experience in the American language; your writing is a well-packaged product because the foreignness you're selling is domesticated and pitched to an exact niche market. The immigrant who came to the US as an adult remains forever tongue-tied and can never get rid of foreign syntax. You are caught in your mixed feelings—excessive gratitude towards your new homeland and recognition of your own non-belonging to it, your embarrassment and your trickster's joy. The packaging of metaphors and experiences is harder for you; you are forever caught up in a web of mixed feelings, like old slapstick comedians. On the one hand, you are sometimes too enthusiastic for your second homeland, against all odds, on the second hand, you are too embarrassed of your failure to belong, on the third hand, too long-winded and grateful for little things, on the fourth hand, easily offended by the minutia of foreign life, on the fifth hand, clumsy and frazzled, not cool and collected, on the sixth hand, "those (immigrant) mental states sprout additional forelimbs all the time," writes Nabokov's immigrant super achiever about his less successful fellow-émigré, Timofei Pnin. Immigrant is a centipede (sorokonozhka) with many aching limbs.

When we, the Soviet refugees, arrived in the US we received short and simple lessons in good American English: avoid Russian long sentences, don't use "perhaps" and impersonal constructions, don't beat around the bush, show your agency. You are responsible for your actions, so just say "I did this and that and that." But in Russian we had a proverb: "I (ia) is the last letter of the alphabet." "No but. And avoid the proverbs. Nobody gets them. But maybe … One more thing: don't ever try to make jokes. You're already funny." Writing in characters helps me to reconcile my Russian and American style, at least provisionally. Zenita, Susana, Svetlana—they caught me unawares. They cross paths throughout this book, occasionally bumping into one another. Together they tell a collective story of the move from inner immigration to actual emigration; a story of double lives and multiple perspectives. Immigrant resilience is built on forgetting and working towards a new start. What will the backward glance accomplish?

I miss Zenita, the child of the 1960s, as I miss my mother's youthful laughter, artful hair updo, crowded beaches and my father's comical badges of the KZBZ and KINO. Zenita, named after the cosmic football team, is the one who wouldn't need to emigrate. She embraced being a young pioneer precisely because of that disturbing alcoholic breath of the ungainly pioneer leader whose shaky finger made an improbably loose knot on her neck during the wonderful rite of passage. Little Zenita tried to show that it hadn't marred the day for her, it was all worth it. And since that moment on she would always like to improve the system from within, try to make it better, not leave it. At the age of nine Zenita would try without much success to be a great figure skater, at least on the parquet floor of her parents' room. She would dream of flying into space making a second home on the Red Planet, like Aelita, the queen of Mars. At eleven, while gaining some interest in the foreign D'Artagnan, she would still follow young Vladimir Ulyanov-Lenin into his underground and write many secret messages calling for a new revolution in milk from an inkwell made of bread. We all liked that story. In one of his underground hideouts or maybe even in a tsarist prison, Lenin was left without pens. All he was given to eat was porridge, milk and bread. He would eat the porridge, for strength, and then he would make a little inkpot out of softened bread and pour milk inside. He would dip his finger into milk and write important revolutionary directives invisible to his prison guards. His addressee would get the precious paper and bring it close to fire in order to read it. Please try this at home. Zenita and I loved that revolutionary writing white-on-white; yesterday's milk on yellowish paper. Now when you bring the paper close to a gas stove (or camp fire), you will see shaky letters with burnt shadows emerge gradually in the middle of the page. Zenita would do well in literature and in math and even won an honorable mention in the Children's

Math Olympics. By age fourteen, high-school Leninism started to bother Zenita and she decided to look for the "true Marx" beyond a few memorized and predigested quotes in the school manual. As she began to dream of a Marxist revolution, she would unwittingly replicate the polemics between Trotskyists and left Socialist Revolutionaries circa 1919. And then came that "class meeting of extreme importance and urgency" in the seventh grade chaired by the director of the school herself and with the whole school board presiding. It was a public renunciation of the "traitors of the motherland" and their allies. The reason for this obligatory official meeting was the departure from the Soviet Union of one of our pupils, Mark, whose family decided to emigrate from the Soviet Union to Israel.

This type of meeting was highly recommended in such cases, but our local officials showed an unusual zeal and initiative. The class master asked all students whose "nationality" in the school ledger was Jewish to stand up and renounce international Zionism and cosmopolitism. There were four or five Jews in our class and a few crypto ones, who didn't count on this occasion. The first student with the last name "Joffe" (I remember this like it was yesterday) volunteered enthusiastically; stood up before his alphabetical turn had come and denounced Zionist cosmopolitan Western propaganda. Zenita and Svetka Goldberg, listed as "Jewish," were next. They just stood up. And said absolutely nothing. She stood with her lips sealed like a partisan. A long uncomfortable silence ensured. A little fidgeting and whisper but mostly silence. The director and the head class mistress were silent too. They tried to say "So?" "Nu?" but then stopped. Everyone was locked in five or ten minutes of silence. It was like a Chekhov play except there was no violin playing in the destroyed garden. The silence continued until one privileged kid, the tall and handsome Misha, son of a university rector and not Jewish at all, stood up and said, "I think we shouldn't be judging Mark so quickly; he is just obeying his parents who are emigrating." Neither Zenita nor Svetlana remembers what happened next. Only this statement saved everyone and somehow allowed the school apparatchiks a face-saving way of cutting the meeting short. At the end Svetka/Zenita shook Mark's hand and this stopped him from bitter tears.

Mark, incidentally, got back in touch ten years later: he was in Canada, studying to be a rabbi. He still remembers that story. Svetka might have started to think emigration at that moment while Zenita took her firm stand for justice inside the country. (Did Svetka neglect to share that story with you? She is always forgetting important things.) Zenita stays focused. The beautiful words about just society, peace, internationalism and love between people have been profaned! Time for more writing in milk, white-on-white, of a different kind. She went to the secret meetings of a tiny grass root group of local dissidents who read smuggled chapters of Alexander Solzhenitsyn's *Gulag Archipelago* and an even more troubling book, *Lolita*, by an unknown émigré writer named Vladimir Nabokov. (Svetka wasn't told about these. The meetings took place not far from the building where they lived, you could get there from their courtyard. Svetka's friend from the literary club, the poet Alexandra Nefetova, went there too but swore to keep a secret from everyone, including Svetka.) Zenita found Nabokov's style too flowery and overwritten for her taste, and the subject matter was disturbing, but some passages were beautiful. Ze-ni-ta wasn't able to finish Lo-li-ta in the one night she was allowed to keep the book. She fell asleep, her one-night stand with Nabokov ended on an early chapter. She did get into Solzhenitsyn and tried to learn more about her grandmother Sonya's experiences in the Gulag too. Zenita loved the Baltic resorts like Zelenogorsk, conquered by the Soviets during the Russian–Finnish war, which still kept large and ornate country houses built by the Finns, that were expropriated by the Soviets, that gave the place a foreign aura. There was also a long sandy beach with dunes and a labyrinthine part there with endless flower beds that housed encouraging slogans made of forget-me-nots, dandelions, bellflowers, chrysanthemums. Unlike Svetka, she resisted falling for Sasha B., whose father was a colonel and who studied French and cut deals with Finnish tourists on the black market.

Zenita couldn't fall for anyone who hasn't read Pasternak and knew even less about Marx and surplus value. It was Svetka who was driven by that adventure of freedom or sometimes just an adventure while Zenita was looking for true love. She was prepared to wait for it. Koktebel charmed her with its purple mists and Sapphic hills. She bought herself a Zenit camera and took nicely framed pictures of Koktebel fences and shadows falling on her and her friends in the wavy sand. She snacked on sundried vobla and listened to many conversations about "leaving," where "leaving" meant leaving for ever. She listened carefully but she had already met Yura, her fellow student in mathematical linguistics at the Pedagogical Institute. He was shy at first and she wasn't sure if he took her seriously. She worried that he might have been seduced by Irka Sidorova, the daughter of a law professor and very well-connected. But then Yura came to Koktebel—she saw him right as she was about to join a line for beer and vobla and asked: "Excuse me, who is next?" "I am next," he said quietly. "Next to you." Yura had many dreams and ambitions of his own, he wanted to study mathematical linguistics to understand cosmic communication or at least to study alternative models of the universe through semiotics, the way it was pioneered at the Tartu School in Estonia. He was tallish with a sparkling dimple on his cheek and seriousness in his grey eyes. It was totally unfashionable in those days to say anything explicit but I would imagine (for I didn't do it and wouldn't have any idea what it would feel like), I could only imagine that they really did whisper "I love you" quietly to each other with the shimmer of the wave. Or maybe they didn't need the shimmer and the words at all. But they did whatever they did putting all ironic distance aside. Of course, Zenita married Yurochka in an understated ceremony in the Palace of Weddings and then suffered from endless reproaches from his relentless Jewish mother. She could do nothing right by her mother-in-law at first, but then they got their own studio apartment, god knows through what connections. In a year or so they made their honeymoon journey through the Crimea from Koktebel to Bakhchisarai, to Chufut Kale, the secret towns of the Karaites. The Karaites were mysterious and mystifying; sometimes they claimed to be the original and most authentic Jews and at other times, when it was inconvenient to be Jews, they claimed not to be. Thus, they didn't pay "Jewish" taxes to the Russian tsar and were not rounded up by the Nazis during the Second World War. They left striking tomb stones with ruined Hebrew letters and a patina of forgotten history. (All of that is another story.) Image 1: Zenitochka in her risqué Polish bikini and Yura stooping shyly and pressing her tightly to his hairy chest. Image 2: Karaites rocks, bifurcating cracks around the letter Hey.

In the stagnating 1980s, talk of emigration became background noise in many Jewish households. But Yura's mother had a security clearance and couldn't get an exit visa, and they wouldn't leave without her. Really? Shall we talk about this? No, out of the question. Somehow Zenita never had a visceral urge to leave. She didn't love her job as a school math teacher but she continued with her short writing experiments, short documentary stories from the life of Leningrad yards, prose poems about bleeding autumnal leaves dancing on electric wires and the burned fingers of the Aurora Borealis. (Not so good in English translation.) She stopped with the poems when little Boria was born. And then came glasnost followed by perestroika and life has become merrier, to quote Mayakovsky. Zenita saw the books she read in samizdat in semi-open circulation and she was ready to become an active participant in the time of transition. It was as if her earlier inner immigration now prepared her for open public life. She marched to the Palace Square to face the tanks in August 1991. In the nineties she went for many public discussions and even published her journalism and photographs. Teaching kids was becoming more interesting even though it paid less and less. But as the 1990s went downhill after 1996–1998, Zenita started to experience something of a midlife crisis. Borechka was doing some start-up business in high school, Yura appeared distanced and tired, and she was drawing blanks on her own writing. True, they took lovely vacations abroad, to Europe and even to Turkey, but they were only tourists there, learning more about themselves with interesting backdrops for the family pictures. It's during that time, in 1998 or so, that Zenita met a visiting professor from America, glamorous Susana-Svetlana, who looked a bit like her only her gait was very different. She walked like a person who needed to leave free space around her, to lean on nobody, to take her own direction. Yet there was something ungrounded about her too. She traveled light and cringed when called Svetka by strangers and refused to add any suffix of endearment to her name. But Zenita felt that Svetlana lived in an enchanted expanding world. Her old-fashioned Leningradian Russian tinged with a foreign intonation turned every sentence into a dangling inquiry. It didn't occur to her to ask Svetlana if she was happy in love. It was clear that she found life with a capital "L." That night, Zenita argued as usual with her son Bor-ka who brought some new "brands" home, she left Yura watching disturbing news on TV, put on her Yugoslav robe, and then lay facing the old yellow wallpaper of her ex-Soviet bedroom and thinking what it would be like to be Svetlana and dream in a foreign room painted "Toscana red." She cried a little for her possible lives but then counted sheep like her mother told her "count the sheep and visualize it, one, two, three, white, grey, black" and fell asleep touching Yura's beloved body ever so slightly.

In the morning Zenita put some eye cream to cover her blues. For the blues are just a part of life. Zenita remained grounded and strong. Sometimes, she looks over my shoulder with reproach and disbelief as I stare at the ceiling, letting angry short circuits of thought overwhelm my best ideas and sparks of wonder amidst scattered books and chocolate foils. "You are the one who got all our chances …" I know, in my heart of hearts, that Zenita is right and without her this book would never be written. Svetlana Boym, the scholar and writer, seems to be the most accomplished of us all, but the traces of the other girls with unfinished fates occasionally bleed into her organized prose. For a while Svetlana managed to conduct an experimental symphony with all of us. She embraced this syncopic experience of exilic sensual details, of life without a synthesis; resisting blinding ideologies and ready-made administrative thinking and never ceasing to explore new destinations for emigration. But then the fickle Fortuna played a trick. First Svetlana broke her leg walking casually by the Charles River. She took many pictures of teasing shadows on the rippled surface of the river and wondered what was really broken inside her and what phantom limb was let loose. She decided as always to play it light, to co-create with the accident and not make a bigger deal out of her midlife fall than need be. And then her long-term American marriage broke just as accidentally as the limb and somehow that affected her whole foundation. She learned the paradox that for the adventure of mobility you needed a strong and stable skeleton. Mobility and security are provided by the same joints. She grappled with uncertainty most of her life but always with the sense of personal security and companionship existing somewhere in the background, whether real or imaginary. Confronting insecurity and uncertainty in midlife without that energy of immigrant resilience seemed an insurmountable task. At that moment the last of our imaginary creatures sprung into being, a desperate adventuress named Lana-Ilanka, a woman of indefinite foreign origins, a Jewish cosmopolitan, a globe trotter and coy virtual dater, also known as Ilanka66 ("hi gorgeous. LOL.") She described herself as a "beautiful, somewhat intelligent, college teacher and artist." Ilanka, open-minded, glamorously melancholic, easy to ichat with and sometimes to "meet for coffee," was the least happy of my bunch. Ilanka suddenly realized that after thirty years in America, she remains a stranger here and not only to herself.

This latest delayed shock of immigration was the hardest one to take. She deserved to belong already, never mind the "cute" identifiable accent. Do you always have to answer the question "Where are you from" that a complete stranger imposes on you? She kept trying to pass for a hyphenated-native, or something like that; just a person with a slightly unusual biography, but for most people she remained an "exotic" woman, fun for dating but perhaps too unusual for life. It's easy to be attracted to foreigners and then drop them as quickly as you pick them up; they are not a part of your family and never would be. Ilanka began to feel like a resident alien in her near-native Boston with her best friends dispersed all over Europe and New York. Ilanka was a distant cousin of the adventurous Suzanne-Susana. Only Susana was young, enjoyed her creative defamiliarization and solitude with a sense of security. Instead of this creative solitude when you're in dialogue with yourself and others, Ilanka felt isolated and unspeakably lonely. Solitude is when you are in conversation with your best daimons; loneliness is when no such dialogue seems possible. Our slender Ilanka66 with the great haircut and cool glasses looked so good on paper but proved to be the weakest link in life. Zenita, Susana, Ilanka—they took me by surprise. I didn't plan for them to come forth. Until the moment of crisis, Susana and Zenita didn't talk back to me and Ilanka seemed just my virtual dating avatar. Each name is a limb with its own phantom pleasure and pain. They have their own bifurcating lives that often elude me. We are independent but a little co-dependent too. We change roles and play musical chairs and sometimes there is a mishap, a gap, a fall. And there is that nameless girl who liked to play hide-and-seek because she trusted that whenever she hid there would be for sure someone seeking her.

Maybe together, the collective of imaginary siblings can help the single child? I read that the best cure for phantom pain is the mirror method, which allows you to confront the wandering limbs that haunt us. This book is an attempt at the mirror method. I never wished to assimilate completely and fit into the proverbial American melting pot. Nor did I want to affirm my immigrant identity and the warmth of the displaced community. I hoped for a third way, the knight's move. Not to have to try to assimilate but to have dissimilar others around me to engage in the adventure of living. Persona was a mask in Greek tragedy but wearing that mask wasn't a mere disguise but a revelation of a deeper self. For me personal integrity was always more important than a coherent personal identity. Neither of the two words "integrity" and "identity" translate well into Russian. (There is plenty of "soul" and "truth", of course.) Perhaps that kind of integrity without full integration can be found in a passionate dialogue with others through teaching and research and our last imaginary homeland—nostalgia for world culture? In my graduate school days as I walked through immigrant districts of the city and then took the crowded subway to the university, it never occurred to me that it was an ivory tower or some kind of free autonomous zone. They were interconnected spaces, one leading into another like the corridors of the communal apartment and the railway station in my dreams. The questions of human suffering, displacement, world wonder, human communication didn't seem to me merely academic. My study helped me make sense of my immigrant experience and to share it with others. If anything, the relationship between life and research seemed too continuous. Ivory Tower hasn't always been a pejorative term; it comes from the lover's discourse in the Song of Songs: Your throat is like an ivory tower. It's about the beauty of the beloved body, an amorous architecture of the cosmos. It's the prudish nineteenth century and the anti-intellectualism that made the term pejorative. Yet it is true that there are scholars who devote themselves to the narrow confines of disciplinary knowledge, but in both of my homelands, the USSR and USA, the term was too frequently abused in order to attack intellectuals and critical thinkers. So, I will stick to the lover's tower, shaped in an avant-garde spiral like the tower of Tatlin. In the face of enormous inequality in the United States (and less acknowledged, in the Soviet Union and Russia as well), the ivory tower is not the most dangerous place. I know how unpopular it is to observe this, but in fact it is the popular culture in the United States that is far from democratic and has been created by the entertainment industry that is way more economically and politically powerful than a bunch of artists, scientists and academics.

Jargons of exclusion are not the sole property of academia nor its only characteristic. Today there is more danger that a university would become yet another corporate tower losing its relative independence and focus on research and teaching. Once, while finishing *Another Freedom* about five years ago, and being particularly annoyed at the bureaucratic agendas, I decided to put a quote from Tocqueville's *Democracy in America* on my office door at the Barker Center at Harvard. A great admirer of American political institutions and a critic of American mentality, Tocqueville observed the paradoxes of striving individualism and conformity:

"I know of no country in which there is so little independence of mind and real freedom of discussion as in America."

I couldn't anticipate the reaction to my quote. Next day I was told by the building supervisor to remove the quote. "Why?" I asked suspecting censorship. "It violates the building design," explained the supervisor. "We like office doors to look uniform."

Yet whenever I fall into nostalgic non-conformism, I remember the wise words of my former mentor, writer and critic Barbara Johnson, who gave me a life lesson after I got a job at Harvard. "Stop speaking about anti-establishment, Svetlana. Now, you're the establishment." She had a good sense of irony, and I see her lips crack in a wistful smile. One just has to learn to live with some fractures, co-create with what's given and not flee from one's ideals at the first misfortune. Not all roads not taken are better than the roads taken. Emigrate when needed. Regret nothing. I happened to live through many declarations of the "ends of": the end of history, the end of art, the end of the Soviet Union, etc., some more real than others. That's probably why I have such difficulty with closures. The end of the Soviet Union and its satellite states didn't bring with it the "end of history"; in fact, history gushed out as if from an open wound. And capitalism didn't simply win the game, democracy is not exactly on the rise in the world, either, and we are not sure who (if anyone) won the Cold War. As for the end of the "snail world" (i.e. the non-digital retro-existence of senses and face-to-face encounters), it hasn't occurred yet either. There was a way in which the inner emigration in my childhood and the escape into a virtual universe of literature prepared me for the digital existence and virtual dating. However, I remained a "digital immigrant"; not a digital native, but after my experiences of border crossing, I embraced my digital non-resident alien status with pleasure. One can still remain a trickster and move sideways, making an alternative path in the virtual world without sacrificing the sentient world. As I am about to put an end to this tale of "the end of immigrations," PBS is airing a program about another "end of ..." as if mocking me with my desire for closure. This time it's not about "the end of history" or "the end of art," but something more ambitious—the end of homo sapiens—that can be translated as an "inquiring human." Yuval Noah Harari, the author of the new book, *Sapiens: A Brief History of Humankind*, predicts that in the not so remote future "sapiens," knowing won't be any longer attached to a human but to a wise machine or to a new caste of super-reach cyborgs of inhuman longevity. Unlike in the era of my childhood, most futuristic thinking today leans towards the dystopian, rather than the utopian, although they often overlap. The nice part of the title is that "the history of humankind is "brief," and we will soon be a retro specie of humorous reflection. Human immigrants. Of course, this might be another foreboding scientific fairy tale. One thing the Soviet experience taught me—to be a good reader of fairy tales; not to merely run behind hunky Komsomol leader Ivan the Fool in the search for his explosive Fire Bird, but to map the migrating plots and porous textures of fear and wishful thinking itself. The fairy tales of this book are now about to begin.

Svetka, age four and a half, wanted to be a Little Red Riding Hood. She got dressed like a fairy tale girl and went for the New Year celebration for kids at her mother's workplace. And there she saw an old doctor on stage with a needle, human size. She didn't want the kids to suffer pain. "Children, we've been deceived! screamed Svetka, disrupting the party. "This is not a show, this is a hospital!" Zenita, age ten, dreamed of a true Kosmos. She drew pictures of rockets, looked at photographs of animals and people who traveled into space and wanted to see a real sputnik—which in Russian means both a satellite and a life companion. And then she learned that the little dog Laika sent by comrade Khrushchev into outer space never came back to earth. And what's worse, it was arranged as a one-way trip all along. Children, we've been deceived! Kosmos as we knew it no longer exists, or perhaps it has never existed. And there is ageing Susana, gathering stones with bifurcating veins in the Crimean mist in the ruins of the twentieth-century dreams and military debris. Let's remember what we've tried to forget, kids. Let's multitask with clouds. Let's play with a different fire.

ACKNOWLEDGMENTS

I would like to express my deep thanks to Musa and Yuri Goldberg for the honor of editing these works of Svetlana's and to Svetlana for writing them and for her friendship. I would particularly like to thank Natal'ya Strugach and Maria Vassileva for their respective contributions to one of the stories here ("Tearing Away") and for their permission to publish it in this volume. I wish also to extend my thanks to Tamar Abramov. Finally, thanks to my friend Irina for boundless encouragement.

INDEX

Adamo, Salvatore 62, 89, 90
Aibolit, Doctor 17, 18, 20, 29, 36, 37
Aksyonov, Vasily 73, 75
Almodovar, Pedro 128
Angry Young Men 35
Arendt, Hannah 138

Baba Yaga 36
Bagristsky, Vsevolod 52
Beatles 7, 74, 120
Berkeley, George 10, 11, 13
blockade, Leningrad 26, 46, 64
Bolshoy Prospekt (Avenue) 55, 56, 58, 59, 62, 86
Bonoparte, Napoleon 85, 93, 100
Borges, Jorge Luis 119, 127, 129
Borodino 83
Boston 14, 55, 66, 86, 103, 104, 123, 125, 126, 128, 129, 133, 134, 139, 151
Boym, Konstantin 66, 121, 123
Brezhnev, Leonid 8, 11, 22, 78, 92, 95
Brodsky, Joseph 44, 58
Bronze Horseman 132
Brothers Grimm 18, 20, 28, 48, 49
Brothers Karamazoff 60
Brown, Clarence 67

Chaliapin, Feodor 79
Chukovsky, Kornei 20
Communal Apartment 97, 107, 109, 124, 131, 152
Communism 6, 7, 10, 22, 74, 92, 107, 115
Communist Party 6, 34, 81, 82, 95, 117
Connecticut 103, 106, 111
Crimea 10, 63, 74, 119, 121, 137, 147

Day of the Soviet Army 8
Day of the Soviet Aviation 8

Death in Quotation Marks 130
Degas, Edgar 73, 74
Dissidents 45, 139, 146
Don Quixote 120, 130, 141
Dostoevsky, Fyodor 32, 60
Dubrovnik 89

Einstein, Albert 11

Femida, Goddess of Justice 33, 49, 85
Fenway Park 124
flea markets, American 103
Free Philosophical Association 79

Gagarin, Yuri 6, 7, 9
Galeano, Eduardo 2, 3
Genrikovna, Gertruda 46
Great Patriotic War 22
Griboedov, Alexander 51
Gulag 24, 26, 27, 45, 48, 109, 117, 120, 146
Gulag Archipelago 146

Harari, Yuval Noah 154
Harvard University 130
Helsinki Accords 70
Hermitage (Museum) 42
Hitchcock, Alfred 115
House of Culture 17, 18, 22, 26, 34, 36, 37

Ivan the Fool 6, 14, 18, 19,117, 131, 154

Jesus Christ Superstar 74
Jewish Family and Children Service (JFS) 124

Karaklajić, Radmila 89
Karpovka River 56, 58, 132
Kazakhstan 46

Kharms, Daniil 64
Kirov Avenue, Kirovsky Avenue 85
Kirovsky Prospekt
Kirov Park of Culture and Leisure 91
KGB 45, 46, 72, 129
Kodak 105
Koktebel 66, 119, 121, 147
Komsomol (Communist Youth Party) 66, 81, 154
Korolev, Sergei 14
Kosmos 6, 10, 13, 154, 155
Khrushchev, Nikita 21, 44, 73, 109, 154
Kulak 118
KZBZ 26, 115, 144

Lenin, Vladimir 11, 33, 44, 59, 71, 93, 97, 131, 144, 145
Lermontov, Mikhail
Leningrad (St Petersburg/Petrograd) 2, 9, 11,12, 13, 22, 23, 24, 25, 26, 29, 30, 34, 42, 44, 45, 46, 50, 59, 60, 64, 65, 66, 85, 86, 89, 95, 96, 103, 107, 111, 115, 121, 123, 128, 129, 131, 132, 133, 134, 137, 141, 148, 149
Leningrad State Pedagogical Institute 120
Leningrad University 10, 119
Llull, Raimon 129
Lolita 20, 146
Lot's wife 131

Madrid 78, 120, 128, 129
Magomaev, Muslim 91, 92
Mandelshtam, Osip 20, 31, 118, 119
March of the Aviators 8, 23
Marx, Karl 61, 131, 145, 147
Marxist-Leninist 10, 131
Mayakovsky, Vladimir 60, 124, 148
Mayoro, Nikolai 52
Merwin, W.S. 67
Military Naval Academy 94
Morozov, Pavlik 29, 117
Moscow 66, 67, 71, 79, 82, 83, 96, 111, 121, 123, 133, 137
Multitasking with Clouds 139

Nabokov, Vladimir 139, 146
Nazis 148
Nefetova, Alexandra 146
Neva embankment 59, 89, 94
Nevsky Prospekt 99, 100
New York City 86, 87, 94, 98, 151
Nietzsche, Friedrich 55, 89, 90, 95, 98
Nostalgia 1, 58, 64, 67, 106, 119, 120, 128, 134, 135, 139, 141, 152

October Revolution 44, 72, 79
Odysseus 119
Okudzhava, Bulat 57, 72, 73, 75
Olympic Games 95, 96, 123
Order of the Red Banner of Labor 50
OVIR (Office of Visas and Registration) 76, 77

Palace of Culture 27, 47
Perrault, Charles 20
Peter and Paul Fortress 89
Petrograd (Leningrad/St Petersburg) 26, 59
Petropavlovsky Street 56
Phantasmagorias of History 139
Pioneer 21, 34, 35, 36, 59, 117, 124, 140, 141, 144
Pizarnik, Alejandra 141
Prague (Spring) 22, 133, 139
Pravda 7, 45, 61, 111
Proust, Marcel 1, 3
Pushkin, Alexander 32

Radio Mayak 82
Red Riding Hood 17, 18, 19, 20, 21, 25, 28, 29, 36, 47, 117, 120, 154
Red Square 71
Refusenik 63, 76, 123
Reid, Thomas Mayne 118
Rodari, Gianni 28, 48
Russia 31, 46, 64, 66, 67, 83,131, 132, 133, 134, 135, 137, 138, 139, 142, 152

Shklovsky, Victor 1, 11, 142
Solzhenitsyn, Aleksandr 146

Soviet Ministry of Internal Affairs 76
Soviet Union 2, 6, 14, 20, 24, 27, 50, 64, 70, 71, 78, 82, 86, 115, 116, 122, 124, 130, 133, 134, 145, 152, 153
Spain 120, 127, 128, 129, 142
Spanish Civil War 120
Sputnik 5, 48, 59, 115, 154
Stalin, Joseph 21, 22, 23, 24, 44, 46, 74, 79
St. Isaac Square 132
St Petersburg (Leningrad/Petrograd) 2, 45, 58, 59, 65, 79, 134, 137
Subjective idealism 10

Tatlin, Vladimir 152
Temple of our Savior in Blood 98
Tereshkova, Valentina 13
The Future of Nostalgia 67, 134, 141
The Three Musketeers 33, 118
Tocqueville, Alex de 153
Tolstoy, Leo 26, 47

Trubachev, Vasek 29
Tsiolkovsky, Konstantin 14
Tsar Nikolai II 46
Tsvetaeva, Marina 130

USA 128, 142, 152
USSR 5, 22, 62, 66, 78, 128, 152

Velvet revolution 133
Voice of America 74, 78
Vysotsky, Vladimir 39, 40, 73, 75

Winter Palace 46, 78

Young Pioneers 59, 141

Zelenogorsk 51, 53, 146
Zenit (Leningrad/St Petersburg) 115, 117
Zhukovsky, Vassily 116

www.ingramcontent.com/pod-product-compliance
Lightning Source LLC
Chambersburg PA
CBHW061841300426
44115CB00013B/2461